Creating the Strategy

Winning and Keeping Customers in B2B Markets

Rennie Gould

KoganPage

LONDON PHILADELPHIA NEW DELHI

First published in Great Britain and the United States in 2012 by Kogan Page Limited

120 Pentonville Road	1518 Walnut Street, Suite 1100	4737/23 Ansari Road
London N1 9JN	Philadelphia PA 19102	Daryaganj
United Kingdom	USA	New Delhi 110002
www.koganpage.com		India

© Rennie Gould, 2012

The right of Rennie Gould to be identified as the author of this work has been asserted by him in accordance with the Copyright, Designs and Patents Act 1988.

ISBN   978 0 7494 6614 5
E-ISBN   978 0 7494 6618 3

British Library Cataloguing-in-Publication Data

A CIP record for this book is available from the British Library.

Library of Congress Cataloging-in-Publication Data

Gould, Rennie.
  Creating the strategy : winning and keeping customers in B2B markets / Rennie Gould.
    p. cm.
  Includes index.
  ISBN 978-0-7494-6614-5 – ISBN 978-0-7494-6618-3   1. Industrial marketing.   2. Strategic planning.   3. Customer relations.   I. Title.
  HF5415.1263.G68 2012
  658.8'02–dc23
                                                              2012008073

Typeset by Graphicraft Limited, Hong Kong
Printed and bound in India by Replika Press Pvt Ltd

For Carol, Vanessa, Jamie and Harriet

CONTENTS

Introduction

What is this book about?

In this book, business performance is defined as the ability to *win* and *keep* customers. It therefore argues that the creation of sales and customer strategy provides the route to outstanding business performance in B2B markets.

The book begins by discussing how strategy is created through strategic direction, customer strategy, the value proposition and sales process, and then moves into how strategy is implemented through business purpose, people and performance and development and motivation. In this way, it brings together all the essential elements of both strategy creation and strategy implementation, and introduces new and powerful techniques to the areas of customer targeting, the creation of customer value, and in more effective ways of engaging with customers. Additionally, the book introduces new ways of looking at leadership, organization structure and performance management.

This book argues that the creation and implementation of strategy is ultimately a management responsibility, and it therefore emphasizes the role of management during each step of strategy creation and strategy implementation, putting the creation of strategic customer relationships at the forefront of management thinking. Given that the most important customer relationships in B2B markets are created through personal interactions, this book emphasizes the importance of the direct sales role and the need for highly skilled sales professionals.

Additionally, this book argues that the implementation of sales and customer strategy should provide the organizing rationale and operational blueprint for the whole organization.

Who is this book for?

The book is essentially a practitioner's toolkit of ideas and techniques in sales and customer strategy – a complete manual for leaders and managers wanting to create and manage strategy in their organization. For the first time in one volume, this book brings together all that is necessary to create outstanding business performance in B2B markets to provide essential reading for all managers and business leaders involved in either creating or managing strategy for their organization. This will include managing directors, general managers, marketing directors, sales directors and sales managers, all of whom are responsible for the business performance of their organizations. The book will be relevant to those working in both small and large organizations, but particularly for those organizations that have grown to the point where they now require more structured thinking in all aspects of sales, customer strategy and commercial organization. Additionally, this book will be relevant to those studying for postgraduate degrees in management, business or marketing, particularly in the areas of B2B marketing or strategic sales management.

How does this book work?

This book is based on management theory but augmented by many years of consultancy experience with organizations in the B2B marketplace such as AXA Insurance, Mercedes-Benz, Royal Mail and Pirelli. This client work has led to the development of a unique and powerful framework that brings together all the factors involved in creating outstanding business performance in the B2B marketplace. This framework forms the structure of the book – the *Business Performance Value Chain*. The book is full of examples, exercises and case studies and is based on a learning and development process proven in many consultancy assignments with clients from most industry sectors.

First, the book looks to *stimulate awareness* of the various issues affecting business performance in B2B markets and of the various techniques that are available to address them. Secondly, through examples and further explanation, it aims to *create understanding* of how these issues and techniques can come together. Thirdly, the process goes on to *generate insights* into what this understanding means for the organization's specific situation in its own marketplace. And finally, the book seeks to *inspire action* by providing a route map and next steps for leaders and managers to follow.

A further objective of the book is to demystify some of the more academic areas of business strategy and to make them more accessible to the business practitioner. The tools and techniques outlined in this book are therefore meant to be used in the real world of sales and customer strategy, and are designed for the purpose of improving organizational effectiveness and business performance.

PART ONE
Sales and Customer Strategy

Sales and customer strategy in B2B markets

01

The importance of sales and customer strategy

The premise of this book is that for organizations operating in the B2B environment, the *winning* and *keeping* of customers is of strategic importance and is fundamental to overall business performance. The creation and implementation of sales and customer strategy must therefore take centre stage in terms of both management thinking and management actions.

This has always been important but is becoming increasingly so, as Professor Nigel Piercy of Warwick Business School outlines in his book, *Strategic Customer Management*:

> The front end of our companies is moving into an era of strategic customer management. The sales organization is becoming a strategic imperative rather than a tactical tool.
>
> For many companies, the strategic management of customers and customer relationships has become a higher priority than conventional marketing activities, which is why we are already seeing major organizations transferring resources from marketing to strategic sales and account management initiatives to achieve better alignment and to achieve the goals of business strategy.
>
> There is a growing consensus that traditional approaches to marketing and sales are doomed to fail, and in particular that the shaping of the selling function has become a strategic corporate issue, requiring clarity about the new sales role, new structures and new management approaches.
>
> The conclusion to which we are drawn is that increasingly the ability of companies to achieve competitive superiority and enhanced business performance through the way they manage customer relationships is a core capability, but one which has been largely ignored by conventional sales and marketing thinking.

This book therefore takes as its overall rationale the strategic nature of customer relationships in the determination of business performance to address such questions as:

- What do we want the business to achieve?
- How do we translate this overall vision of the future into practical objectives and activities?
- In what ways will we measure and acknowledge success?
- How can we create unique customer value from our product and service offering?
- Which customers and prospects represent the best opportunities for business growth?
- How should we deliver our value proposition to our target customers?
- How should we organize the business to deliver customer satisfaction and loyalty?
- What are the roles and responsibilities of both leadership and management in ensuring our success?
- How do we generate a sense of purpose that guides the organization?
- What roles do culture and values have in shaping our behaviour?
- What kind of people do we need to deliver our sales and customer strategy?
- How do we motivate and develop our organization to ensure optimum business performance?

The central role of the sales organization in creating and developing customer relationships in the B2B marketplace is of crucial importance. This book therefore emphasizes this direct sales role and looks in detail at those high-level sales skills and techniques necessary for success.

The importance of sales and customer strategy is not only confined to customer-facing activities and roles; it must also inform all other areas and activities within the B2B organization. In doing so, sales and customer strategy must succeed where other business and management initiatives have failed.

Marketing was going to put the customer first. It was going to organize the business around creating customer value and profit. Unfortunately, in many cases marketing only created marketing departments that effectively said to the rest of the organization: 'Leave the customer to us, just get on and do your own job.' As a result, marketing never really assumed the strategic role it should have attained and did not create the vision and organizing rationale that such a position would have achieved.

Then there was *customer relationship management (CRM)*. CRM was going to revolutionize the business world by bringing together in one place all elements of customer information and making this detailed and up-to-date customer information readily available across the whole organization. This sharing of all customer information would then in some way lead to the optimum management of all customers, providing them with both the services and the relationship they deserved.

Unfortunately, however, CRM has often failed to deliver on these lofty promises and in many cases has left organizations with hugely expensive investments in hardware and software that have yet to pay for themselves. A much more serious issue is that CRM has in many cases created a barrier between the organization and the customer, with customers left feeling remote and removed from those organizations they previously felt close to, relegated to bit-part players dangling on the end of a phone to some Indian call centre. Such organizations appear happy to hide behind processes and technology that keep their customers at arm's length – hardly a move to create and develop customer relationships.

So what about *business strategy*? Strategic thinking by the big cheeses at the top of the organization was going to result in a 'vision' that would guide the organization to the Promised Land. But apart from earning the McKinseys of this world exorbitant fees, all this strategic visioning seemed to do was to create some cute PR and a series of meaningless platitudes that meant very little to the guy on the shop floor or in the back office.

So why should *sales and customer strategy* be any different? In the B2B marketplace, unlike in B2C, organizations can usually identify each of their customers individually and can therefore enter into individual relationships with them. As a consequence, it is much easier to organize the business around meeting the requirements and expectations of customers in the B2B marketplace. *Creating the Strategy: Winning and keeping customers in B2B markets* aims to finally address the above issues by putting the customer and the customer relationship at the forefront of business thinking and organizational design. *In this way, sales and customer strategy drives all other aspects of business strategy.*

The Business Performance Value Chain

The *Business Performance Value Chain* is central to the overall philosophy and process followed in this book. This unique and powerful framework puts the winning and the keeping of customers at the forefront of all strategic thinking to generate outstanding business performance. The framework is responsible for introducing all the elements involved in the creation of sales and customer strategy and for generating the essential insights that drive all activities and behaviour within the organization.

The whole process consists of a series of interlinked elements that must all come together in a coordinated way to create outstanding business performance. Without a powerful sales and customer strategy, management actions would take place in a vacuum and would not create any meaningful commercial activity. Similarly, without the necessary high-performance culture and supportive management environment, sales and customer strategy would not be provided with the opportunity to succeed.

FIGURE 1.1   The Business Performance Value Chain

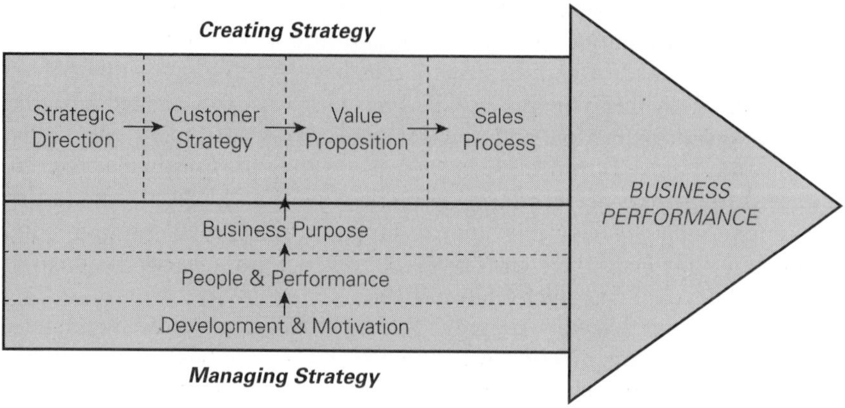

The role of management

This book puts the responsibility for creating and managing sales and customer strategy firmly in the hands of management. It is management who need to ensure the organization is focused on the key activities and processes required to satisfy customer requirements and expectations. It is also management who need to create the overall organizational environment required for success.

The primary role of management at the forefront of strategy is recognized in this framework. In Part Two: Creating Strategy, the requirement for management to create an overall *strategic vision* is the first element examined, and in Part Three: Managing Strategy, the requirement for management to provide an overall sense of *business purpose* also comes first. In this way, leadership and management assume the ultimate responsibility for creating and managing strategy.

Business performance

As this book is concerned with sales and customer strategy in B2B markets, we ultimately define business performance as the result of all the efforts to generate revenue and profits from customers. There are of course many ways of defining business performance and they will be explored in detail in Part Three.

Sales and customer strategy emphasizes the fundamental importance of winning and keeping customers through the creation and development of customer relationships. Ultimately it is the revenue and profit from these relationships that will enable the organization to survive and prosper. The Business Performance Value Chain therefore provides a means to this end by identifying those aspects of sales and customer strategy that must come together to create organizational performance and business success.

Creating strategy

In Part Two, the Business Performance Value Chain identifies the elements in creating the strategy. It starts with *Strategic direction*, which incorporates the overall vision of the organization and its overall goals. This strategic direction provides the overall aiming point for the whole organization and provides the context for the other elements of sales and customer strategy.

Secondly, *Customer strategy* brings together an understanding of the customer in order to identify how they buy and how they make buying decisions. This part of strategy creation also considers the question of customer importance and customer priorities and how these inform the kinds of relationships that the organization wishes to create with different categories of customer.

Thirdly, *The value proposition* looks at the scope of the organization's total product and service offering and how this forms the basis of the organization's unique customer value proposition and competitive positioning. Finally, the most effective ways of engaging with different categories of customer is explored in *The sales process*.

Managing strategy

In Part Three, the Business Performance Value Chain examines the nature of the management role to ensure that strategy is given the best possible chance to succeed. In *Business purpose*, we begin by looking at how management provides this sense of purpose to guide all areas of the organization, together with those elements of culture and values that form the organizational glue needed to keep the organization on track. This section firmly places the responsibility for creating an overall environment of success in the hands of management.

In *People and performance*, we look at the various ways that business performance can be defined and the levers that management have available to influence how the organization performs against all of these measures. This section then goes on to consider the roles that people will need to take in order to deliver the strategy, and what these people will need to be good at. The various options for structuring the organization to facilitate the delivery of sales and customer strategy are also considered, together with the creation of an *Organizational Blueprint* that identifies what this strategy means for the rest of the organization.

In Part Three we also examine the techniques of *Development and motivation*. This will ensure that we create and maintain a high-performance organization that brings together the requirements and expectations of the organization with the needs and desires of the individuals and groups that work within it.

In Part Four, we look at how management can create a high-performing organization by examining some lessons from consultancy and organizational change, and by bringing them together into an overall framework for management action.

In this final section, we also take a look at *The Art of War*, a 2,000-year old treatise on military strategy, to identify what insights it might produce for sales and customer strategy.

Workshop tested

The tools and techniques introduced in this book have been tested in workshops with executives and managers from many different types of organization operating within the B2B environment, and have been proven to create outstanding sales performance. Many of the techniques and frameworks have been derived from the latest thinking in business strategy and management, but have often been adapted to provide specific guidance for sales and customer strategy in the B2B environment. Many other techniques and frameworks introduced by the Business Performance Value Chain are new and have never before been seen in print.

The book follows a logical structure, by first examining how strategic sales strategy is created and then examining how such activity should be managed. It is meant to be a learning resource to stimulate thinking around the reader's own sales and customer issues and opportunities, so that the reader can develop their own strategies that reflect their own competitive environment. The combination of practical experience and the latest academic thinking found in this book will enable readers to find their own answers to their specific sales and customer questions and will enable them to create outstanding business performance in their own organizations.

Self-assessment questionnaire

At the end of this chapter is a self-assessment questionnaire designed to help readers identify some of the most important issues they have in creating and managing sales and customer strategy. The self-assessment is based on the *Business Performance Value Chain* and therefore follows the overall structure of the book.

The questions under each heading are designed to stimulate your thinking and to raise your awareness of some of the most important topics that are addressed in each chapter of this book. You can of course do the assessment at any time, but it might be useful to complete it before reading the book and again at the end to verify your answers. Chapter 9, on *implementing strategy*, will then provide some guidance about how to tackle the issues you have identified.

There are no right or wrong answers. The scoring system is simply a mechanism to help you identify your areas of priority.

The sales and customer strategy self-assessment

Objective of the self-assessment

The purpose of this self-assessment is to help readers identify some of the most important issues they have in *creating and managing sales and customer strategy* and in *winning and keeping customers*.

How to use it

For each question, score yourself as follows:

- *Definitely yes* – 4 points
- *Not sure* – 1 point
- *Definitely not* – 0 points

There are no right or wrong answers. The scoring system is simply to help you identify your own priorities.

E-mail me your analysis

If you would like some comments on your analysis and on your intended strategy, please e-mail your completed self-assessment and your strategy to: **rennie@customizeuktraining.com** and I will be delighted to provide my suggestions.

The self-assessment

Strategic vision

1 Has the top team met recently to discuss any aspect of its strategic direction?
2 Does the organization have a clear vision and a set of overall goals that guide all of its actions?

3 Is there a clear understanding of which market or area of the market the organization wants to compete in?

4 Does the organization know how it wants to be perceived in the minds of its customers?

5 Is there a clear understanding of the organization's specific strengths and distinctive competencies, together with an identification of the opportunities and threats facing the organization?

Customer strategy

1 Has the organization identified its key accounts and development accounts?

2 Does it know how these customers make buying decisions?

3 Does it know what the key purchase criteria of these customers are?

4 Does it know who is typically involved in these buying decisions and the role they play in the process?

5 Do detailed customer profiles exist for describing each category of customer?

Value proposition

1 Have you identified all aspects of your total proposition (total product and service offering)?

2 Have you identified those elements of your total proposition where you have competitive advantage?

3 Do you understand how each element of your total proposition can create customer value?

4 Have you prepared different value propositions for different categories of customer?

5 Can all members of your sales team deliver an elevator pitch?

Sales process

1 Does the organization have a defined sales process for its different categories of customer?

2 Does the organization understand the difference between account planning and activity management?

3 Does the organization use account planning to manage its most important customers?

4 Does the organization use the principle of the sales funnel or sales pipeline to manage all other customers?

5 Does the organization use the principle of the sales funnel or sales pipeline to identify where management intervention is required and create its sales forecasts?

Business purpose

1 Does the organization have a clear view of what defines its existence and gives it a reason for being?

2 Is the organization's business purpose (reason for being) in line with its strategic direction (vision and overall goals)?

3 Are the organization's core beliefs and values well understood throughout the organization?

4 Is the organization being led as well as being managed?

5 Is management behaviour consistent with the organization's declared beliefs and values?

People and performance

1 Are sales targets reflective of customer potential rather than previous levels of business?

2 Has the organization translated its sales and customer strategy into an Organizational Blueprint as a means to ensure the whole organization delivers the ideal customer experience?

3 Do all salespeople have the necessary skills, knowledge and behaviours to be successful?

4 Are annual targets broken down into bite-sized chunks?

5 Is performance feedback provided quickly?

Development and motivation

1 Does the organization have a job specification and a competency profile for each sales role?

2 Does the organization have a development plan for each salesperson?

3 Does the organization carry out skills coaching and strategy coaching?

4 Does the organization know the importance of team development?

5 Has the organization identified the key motivators for each of its salespeople?

Self-assessment scoring sheet

	Max Score	Your Score	Comments
Creating Strategy			
Strategic Direction	4		
Customer Strategy	4		
Value Proposition	4		
Sales Process	4		
Total Creating Strategy	16		
Managing Strategy			
Business Purpose	4		
People & Performance	4		
Development & Motivation	4		
Total Managing Strategy	12		
Grand Total Score	28		

PART TWO
Creating
Strategy

In Part Two we will examine how to create sales and customer strategy in order to win and keep customers in B2B markets. As a guiding framework, we will be using the relevant aspects of the Business Performance Value Chain: *strategic direction, customer strategy, the value proposition* and *the sales process*.

The organization's strategic direction provides the essential focus that pushes the organization forward. Its customer strategy identifies those customers that provide the best opportunities for the kind of business the organization wants to win and keep. The value proposition is the totality of the organization's product and service offering and how these elements come together to create customer value. The sales process defines how the organization will engage with its target customers to extract their full business potential and how it will go about creating the appropriate levels of relationship with each category of customer.

FIGURE 2.1 The Business Performance Value Chain: Strategic direction

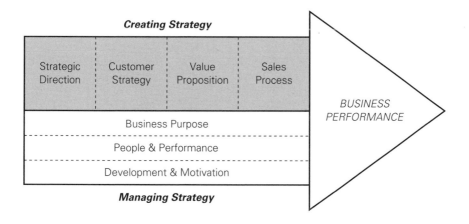

Strategic direction
Where do we want to go as a business?

02

In this first chapter of Part Two, we will examine a number of elements that taken together define *strategic direction*. What we decide in this section will have very important implications for everything we do thereafter, both in terms of creating strategy and then managing it.

As the formulation of strategic direction sets the context for all the other elements involved in creating strategy, it is a concept that requires significant management attention and detailed analysis. Any lack of focus or uncertainty in the organization's downstream aspects of *customer strategy*, *value proposition* and *sales process* can often be traced back to a lack of clarity at this stage of strategy development. As we will see when we consider managing the strategy in Part Three, any lack of strategic direction will also have significant consequences for *people*, *performance* and *development*.

The strategic direction of an organization encompasses a number of different concepts but particularly *vision*, *overall goals*, *core competencies*, *market definition* and *competitive positioning*. The elements of an organization's strategic direction are illustrated in Figure 2.2.

It will be useful at this point to define the various concepts that we are going to consider in this chapter and at various other points in the book. There is a great variation of meaning that exists around terms such as *vision*, *mission* and *goals*, which causes considerable confusion and misunderstanding; therefore, the creation of a common understanding or vocabulary of the various terms used in this section and in the book as a whole will facilitate discussion and understanding. For the purposes of this chapter and for the remainder of the book, we are therefore going to use the following terms in the following ways:

FIGURE 2.2   Strategic direction

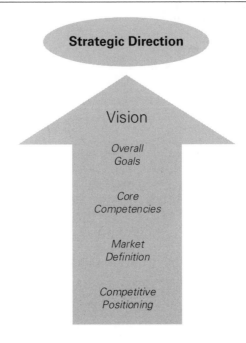

- As previously mentioned, an organization's *strategic direction* summarizes the complementary elements of *vision, overall goals, core competencies, market definition* and *competitive positioning* – all elements that we will consider separately.

- The *vision* is the overall aiming point of the organization. It represents a position in the future that the organization is aiming to reach – a star on the horizon that pulls the organization forward.

- The organization's *overall goals* relate to specific measures that indicate whether the vision is being achieved. Goals are therefore clearly defined and concrete end points of the vision.

- The *core competencies* of an organization are what it does best and therefore define the uniqueness or special attributes of the organization relative to its competition. Core competencies are effectively the same as specific strengths that the organization possesses.

- An organization's *market definition* refers to the particular markets within which it wishes to compete, or defines specific market areas or niches it wishes to target. A market definition therefore specifies the field of play for the organization.

- The *competitive positioning* of an organization is how it wants to be perceived in the minds of its customers within its chosen marketplace. A competitive position specifies a position within the market that the organization intends to call its own.

A note about business purpose

The organization's *business purpose* relates to what defines the organization – what it is all about and what it holds to be important and includes the elements of *culture*, *beliefs* and *values*.

The terms *business purpose* and *mission* mean the same thing, although the term business purpose is preferred in this book to eliminate the confusion that often exists between the similar-sounding terms vision and mission. Although we introduce *business purpose* here, we will explore it in detail in Part Three, Managing Strategy.

The external environment

The strategic direction of the organization cannot be developed in a vacuum, but has to make reference to the external environment the organization faces. The development of strategic direction must therefore analyse this external environment and make certain assumptions about the impact it will have on the organization now and in the future. An analysis of the organization's external environment usually takes into account the elements below.

Political environment

As we have seen in recent years, the political environment can have a significant impact on an organization. Political policies and initiatives impact upon organizations in a variety of ways, from the influence of the overall regulatory framework through to changes in taxation policy and employment legislation. The increasing globalization of world markets has also led to increasing levels of political cooperation and harmonization between countries. These greater levels of political cohesion have increased the effect that political changes and political upheaval in one country can then have on others and have made economies in the West effectively interdependent. Regional differences in political stability are also important aspects for organizations to consider when developing their strategic direction, particularly if this includes an aspect of international business or global expansion.

Economic environment

The relative health of the domestic economy will of course influence an organization's strategic direction. In particular, the impact the economy has on customer demand and on the level of business costs is important. Organizations' growth and investment decisions are particularly sensitive to the perceptions that business leaders have about current and future economic prospects. These decisions are in turn based on the general perceptions that consumers have about future economic prospects. The relatively new discipline of behavioural economics is based on perceptions rather than traditional economic fundamentals.

The increasing globalization of world markets will complicate these issues, as economic conditions in one country can quickly influence conditions in others. Forecasting current and future economic conditions is therefore an important but increasingly difficult task that organizations face. This might suggest that instead of trying to predict an uncertain future, organizations should seek to develop greater levels of organizational flexibility and adaptability to allow them to more readily respond to events that are increasingly outside of their control.

Technological environment

Changes in technology have been a major influence on every aspect of life and will continue to be so. Although it is often difficult to forecast the emergence of new technology and even harder to predict its impact, the changes to every aspect of organizational life brought about by technological innovation can be profound.

Perhaps a major learning point provided by technological innovation has been the impact on organizational capability. It used to be said that technology was merely an enabler, in that it enabled organizations to do existing things better. Increasingly, however, technology has become a game-changer, by creating transformational change in the ways that organizations can engage with their customers and in the ways they can operate internally.

As advances in technology are difficult to predict, this is probably a further argument for leaders and managers to promote flexibility and adaptability within their organizations. This will enable them to respond to such advances, but more importantly to take advantage of the opportunities provided by technology to seize the competitive initiative.

Social and cultural environment

Social and cultural changes occur in society fairly slowly, but they have significant effects over time. Whether these changes relate to demographics, gender, fashion, taste or the basic social fabric of society, they will of course influence the organization's strategic direction.

Technology has had a profound effect on the social and cultural environment, in particular the effect of digital technology on social interaction and communication. A prime example is the sharing of customer perceptions and experiences across all aspects of the digital media, which has had a significant impact on organizations' ability to maintain a specific place in the market and in the minds of their customers.

The development of social networks across the digital media has also increased the importance of customer reviews and recommendations. Amazon in particular have exploited this means of informing customer choice by creating a situation where products will not be purchased from their site until a number of positive customer reviews for that product are already posted. Additionally, the storing of customers' previous browsing and purchasing histories, and the ability to make suggestions based on customers with similar profiles, allows Amazon to offer products they know will be of interest.

It is now almost impossible for an organization to make claims about itself or its products through advertising or other marketing communications that do not tally with actual customer experience. The ability of customers to communicate with each other via digital media has enabled customer experiences to be flashed around the world at the speed of light. This so-called 'word-of-mouse' has become even more influential on customer choice than the organizations' traditional channels of customer communication.

Competitive environment

The nature and scope of competition, particularly the relative strengths and weaknesses of specific competitors that exist within the organization's chosen market, will also have a major bearing on strategic direction. This analysis will influence how the organization chooses to position itself against its key competitors in the minds of its target customers.

Perhaps organizations have historically taken too narrow a view of what constitutes competition, by only recognizing those organizations that compete directly in their own market area. Given that customers have a variety of different options for spending their money, organizations should probably also regard as competitors those that provide a close, alternative choice. In this way, a night watching a DVD at home with a take-away competes with a film watched at a cinema with a meal in a nearby restaurant. Similarly, money spent on a holiday could just as easily be spent on a new sofa for the home.

SWOT analysis

It should be clear from the above that organizations need to monitor the external environment through some form of environmental scanning, and then to bring this information together into a simple format to facilitate an analysis of what it all means for the organization. A SWOT analysis is a popular method of achieving these objectives by bringing together the external *threats* and *opportunities* that exist in the external environment, together with the specific *strengths* and *weaknesses* of the organization.

Figure 2.3 illustrates the four-box nature of the analysis, which allows all the relevant information to be brought together in one place. A SWOT analysis is a *directional technique*, so called because it suggests possible future directions for the organization. There are a number of similar directional techniques used throughout this book, but their objectives are the same – they provide possible strategic options for the organization to consider. In this way, such techniques are designed to augment management thinking, but are no substitute for managerial insight and judgement.

FIGURE 2.3   A SWOT analysis

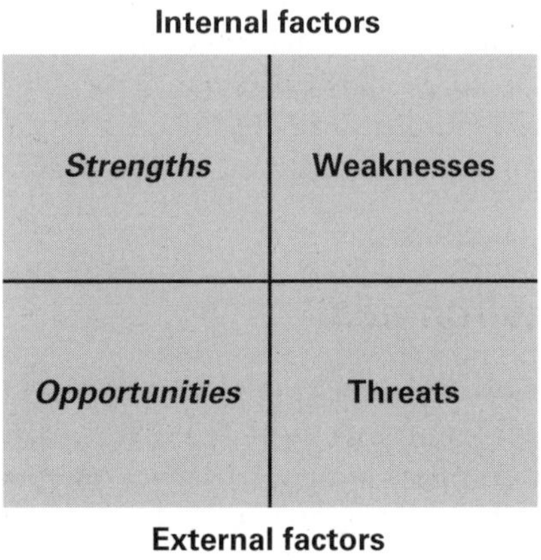

Internal factors

Strengths	Weaknesses
Opportunities	Threats

External factors

Strengths and weaknesses

Strengths relate to what the organization is particularly good at in any aspect of its operations. Ideally, these strengths should be relative to competition, which means that a particular element is only a strength if there is a degree of competitive advantage attached to it.

Weaknesses are the flip side of strengths and relate to things that the organization is not particularly good at in any aspect of its operations. Again, these weaknesses should be relative to competition; that is, a particular element is only a weakness if there is a degree of competitive disadvantage attached to it. Ironically, this could mean that what was initially thought to be a weakness is in fact a competitive strength.

An organization's strengths and weaknesses can be identified by considering the elements outlined below. However, in order to keep the discussion positive, they will be looked at from the perspective of providing potential strengths.

People

The organization's people are a source of strength. People's knowledge, skills, behaviours, experience, know-how and flexibility provide competitive advantages in many areas that the organization can exploit. Additionally, the organization's HR policies and people management processes can be a source of strength, particularly in the areas of recruitment, training, motivation and development – all of which help to develop an organization's flexibility of response.

Specific expertise

The organization may have specific expertise in some area or in some process involved in its business. Such expertise can be found in any area of the organization's operations, including sourcing, manufacturing, distributing, technology, marketing and selling. These specific strengths often define the organization, as they are fundamental to everything the organization does. Such expertise is also referred to as *distinctive* or *core competence* and is something we will explore again in this chapter.

Physical infrastructure and scale

The physical infrastructure, including access to land, buildings, machinery and equipment, is an area where organizational strengths can be found. The sheer size and scale of these elements may impact on such things as geographical reach and market dominance and can allow the organization to undertake certain projects or initiatives that other organizations could not even consider.

Finance

Access to finance is a further potential area of strength and could allow the organization to consider initiatives and operations that other organizations could not. Financial strength may provide the opportunity to acquire other organizations as a way to access new markets and new customers. It can also provide the opportunity to develop and launch new products in new market areas.

In the final analysis, a lack of cash is usually the most important factor that results in business failure. A strong cash flow is therefore another potential financial strength, which can provide some organizations with the ability to survive even in the most difficult economic conditions. Having a strong cash flow can also benefit the organization by allowing it to provide extended credit to customers or better terms to suppliers – both of which could be perceived as competitive strengths.

As far as sales and customer strategy is concerned, the next three elements are particularly important. They are all discussed in outline below, but are explored in more detail in Chapter 3 on customer strategy and Chapter 4 on value proposition.

The total proposition (products and services)

The total proposition represents the entirety of the organization's product and service offering. It is the whole package of everything made available for customers, out of which *customer value* is created.

Organizations often under-estimate the scope and value of their total product and service offering and will therefore under-estimate the full extent of their competitive strength. We will make sure this mistake is not made when we explore the total proposition in more detail later in this section.

An organization's access to markets or customers also forms part of its total proposition – to be explored in more detail later. Access to customers also includes the ability to identify specific customer groups that are more important than others and to engage with each of these groups in a specific and appropriate way via the sales process.

Company or brand image

The image that the organization enjoys in the marketplace may provide a significant source of organizational strength and competitive advantage. In marketing, it is said that *perception is reality*, which means that what customers believe is true for them. Therefore, a positive image in the mind of the customer is a very valuable asset.

A strong image also facilities new product development, entering into new markets, and the development of relationships and partnerships with other organizations. Such an image can also attract good-quality personnel and even promote a general level of goodwill that other organizations cannot achieve.

The customer experience

The concept of the *customer experience* encompasses every aspect of organizational activity that has an impact upon the experience of the customer when engaging with the organization in any way. It includes the experience provided by sales, marketing, delivery, customer service, after-sales and billing. All of these areas provide opportunities for customer interaction (customer touch-points) and therefore provide an organization with a chance to either enhance or diminish the overall customer experience. A positive customer experience will help to create a positive reputation for the organization in the marketplace and will have an important impact on customer satisfaction, loyalty and profitability.

Opportunities and threats

We can now complete the analysis by identifying the external *opportunities* and *threats* facing the organization and bringing them together with the strengths and weaknesses just identified. Opportunities and threats are found by analysing those aspects of the external environment discussed earlier, namely:

- the political environment;
- the economic environment;
- the technological environment;
- the social and cultural environment;
- the competitive environment.

These external issues will affect all organizations in the same competitive marketplace.

Analysing the SWOT

A good SWOT analysis that brings together all the relevant information into one place will almost tell its own story. It will provide a very clear picture of the external issues impacting on the organization and the resources (strengths) it has to deal with them. It will therefore provide important information upon which the strategic direction is largely based.

The strategic direction must thus take into account the outputs from the SWOT in order to:

- mitigate the impact of organizational weaknesses;
- protect the organization against external threats.

But more importantly:

- exploit external opportunities with organizational strengths.

The SWOT analysis and particularly its directional output will be of great benefit in influencing all aspects of the strategic direction, as outlined below.

Vision

Vision is the lead element of the organization's strategic direction and sets the overall agenda for the remaining elements. Vision represents the collective imagination of our organization and its overall aiming point – an idealized place where we would like the organization to be. This vision can be some way off in the future, but its purpose is to inspire the organization to achieve great things.

An organization's vision is often built on the passion and enthusiasm of the organization's original founders or is based on the personal ambitions of the current owners. Either way, vision and passion can be synonymous in providing the essential impetus for the organization. When developing vision, leaders should not feel too restrained by the current situation, as this will constrain any creative thinking. This may be one of the few occasions when leaders of the business are allowed to dream a little and to imagine an idealized future position for their organization. This can be quite difficult for business leaders, who are used to dealing in facts and business realities and might find themselves uncomfortable with this kind of envisioning.

Organizations may never achieve their vision, but its existence will be a constant source of inspiration for the whole organization and will provide an essential focus for all its activities. It will therefore pose the question that the organization needs to address when considering any project or initiative: *Will this action or behaviour take us any closer to achieving our vision?*

Overall goals

The organization's overall goals are specific measures relating to the vision that indicate whether it is being achieved. Goals are therefore clearly defined and concrete end points of the vision. By creating *objectives*, sub-goals can then effectively be produced, where the goal is broken down into a number of specific stepping stones. The achievement of objectives therefore allows the organization to know whether or not it is making demonstrable progress towards its vision and goals.

Core competencies

The strategic direction will be defined in large part by what the organization is particularly good at. These so-called *core* or *distinctive competencies* define the uniqueness or special attributes of the organization, relative to its competition. These competencies have already been discussed under the aspects of strengths and weaknesses when considering the external environment as part of the SWOT analysis. For completeness, they are listed again below:

- people;
- specific expertise;
- finance;
- the total proposition (products and services);
- access to markets or customers;
- company or brand image;
- the customer experience.

As we discovered when considering strengths, an organization's core or distinctive competencies can be found in any aspect of the organization's activities that offers the potential to create competitive advantage.

There is a view held by some business theorists that an organization's core competencies should be the foundation of its strategic direction and subsequent business strategy. The particular view of strategy development that starts from this internal perspective is sometimes referred to as *core competence-based strategy*. This view of strategy development, which looks to exploit the strengths or core competencies of the organization irrespective of the competitive or market environment, runs counter to the traditional view of strategy development, which normally begins with an external market perspective. In this traditional way of developing strategy, the organization is made to fit the environment, whereas by developing strategy from an internal perspective, the external environment is made to fit the organization.

This debate about internal versus external perspectives mirrors the debate that marketers have long engaged in on how marketing strategy should be developed. Having a product orientation or being product-led implies an internal focus, whereas being market-led implies a more external focus. The marketing concept has always preferred the latter approach, but perhaps there is value in both. The practical reality is that strategy is normally developed from a judicious mix of both perspectives – internal and external.

Market definition

Organizations cannot be 'all things to all men'; that is, every organization must decide on the broad areas where it wishes to compete. An organization must focus its firepower in a particular area for maximum effect. Organizations must therefore decide on the particular markets within which they wish to compete, or define even narrower areas or market niches they wish to target. This market definition will limit the areas of activity to those where the organization feels most comfortable and confident, and will outline those areas of the marketplace where the organization will utilize its particular strengths and distinctive competencies to create competitive advantage.

The market definition must be big enough to support the organization's vision and overall goals, but not so big as to lead to organizational resources and focus being spread over too wide an area. If the organization were a car manufacturer, for example, it would have to decide whether to compete in all market segments from small cars to large luxury cars, or only in certain segments such as sports cars or 4×4s. The notion of market definition also has a geographical aspect and relates to those countries where the organization wants to be represented.

Competitive positioning

The issue of *competitive positioning* is very closely related to the issue of market definition. An organization's competitive positioning defines how the organization wishes to be perceived by the marketplace, but more importantly, by its target customers. A statement of competitive positioning therefore specifies how the organization wants to be perceived in the minds of its customers.

Competitive positioning should again be based on the work already undertaken throughout the SWOT analysis, as it relates to where the organization can exploit its particular strengths and distinctive competencies. It is therefore a strategic position that is capable of being defended against competition and also provides opportunities for future growth. The organization may thus take a position based on any aspect of its total product and service offering or on its strengths or distinctive competencies.

The combination of the organization's market definition and competitive positioning specifies the particular place in the market where it seeks the achievement of its vision and overall goals. These issues will also be picked up again in Chapter 4 on the value proposition, when we will look more closely at how elements of the organization's product and service offering create value for customers.

A way of envisioning competitive positioning is by constructing a spidergram as shown in Figure 2.4.

A spidergram illustrates how the organization is currently positioned against customers' *key purchase criteria*. It also illustrates how the organization is positioned against competitors on the same dimensions.

In this example, customers' key purchase criteria can be seen as forming the dimensions on which the spidergram is formed. They include *price*, *delivery*, *after-sales* and so on, with competitive performance ranging from 0 to 10 on the scale. The relative position of the organization versus two

FIGURE 2.4   A spidergram

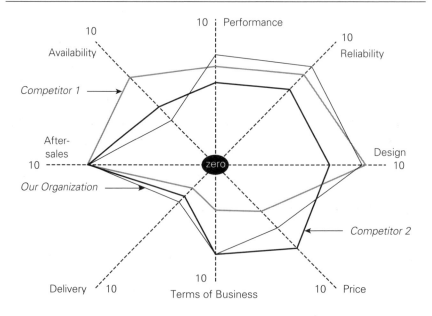

competitors can be seen from where each organization is positioned on the various dimensions. A spidergram can therefore illustrate the current position of organizations in the minds of customers, or it can represent an idealized future position that the organization wants to achieve.

If we assume the spidergram in Figure 2.4 illustrates customers' current perceptions, it can be seen that the organization holds strong competitive positions in *performance* and *reliability*. This might suggest that the organization should identify and target customers who believe that these two factors are the most important in any purchase decision.

Strategic direction and business strategy

Although this book is about sales and customer strategy, the overall strategic direction will have significant implications for the rest of the organization and all other aspects of its business strategy. If we take the view that the products and services offered to customers are ultimately the most important strategic questions facing the organization, then the decisions made in these areas will influence most other decisions and actions across the whole organization. In this way, sales and customer strategy will be at the forefront of management thinking and will drive all other activities of the business. In particular, the vision, overall goals, core competencies, market definition and competitive positioning will influence the organization in all the areas outlined below.

Manufacturing, operations and logistics strategy

Any physical product that the organization makes and distributes, together with any service that the organization makes available to customers, will be influenced by the decisions made concerning the organization's choice of market and its competitive positioning. If the organization decides to occupy a high-quality/high-price/highly exclusive area of the market, then this positioning will have implications for how the organization manufactures and distributes this high-value product. The opposite case, where the organization offers a low-price/low-quality/commodity product, would have very different implications for manufacturing, operations and distribution. The basic point is that manufacturing, operations and logistics must reflect and support the overall strategic direction of the organization.

Financial strategy

The organization's financial strategy and funding requirements will be heavily influenced by the overall strategic direction the organization chooses for itself. If the organization's strategic direction implies a heavy reliance on purchasing raw materials, manufacturing operations, stock holding and logistics, then a corresponding requirement for significant levels of infrastructure and fixed overheads is implied. These activities will put heavy demands upon an organization's funding requirement and cash flow demands.

HR strategy

The structure of the organization and the kind of people it requires will be determined by the organization's strategic direction. This is clear in the case of all sales and customer-facing personnel, but it is also the case that people in other areas of the organization will need to respond to and reflect the requirements of the organization's strategic direction.

We will consider these issues in detail when we look at customer strategy in Chapter 3, particularly the Customer Experience and Organizational Blueprint.

Implications for management

As the strategic direction provides an essential steer for the entire organization, it is an important priority for management. Equally importantly, the existence and implications of this strategic direction need to be communicated across the entire organization to ensure that everyone is aware of what it means for them. Unfortunately, however, an organization's strategy is often its best-kept secret, even from its own people.

Managers sometimes assume that if there are a direction and vision at the top levels of the organization, these will somehow trickle down to all levels as if by magic or through some process of organizational osmosis. The reality is somewhat different; managers need to work very hard to spread the word on a continuous basis through everything they say and through everything they are seen to do. We will look at these issues in detail when we examine culture in Part 3.

Individuals and groups within the organization need to understand how their specific actions and behaviours can contribute towards the achievement of vision and overall goals. It is therefore one of management's key responsibilities to communicate this understanding across the whole organization.

Workshops and case studies

A number of workshops and case studies can be found below. These are designed to help the reader apply some of the techniques discussed in this chapter and to illustrate how organizations have coped with some of the issues raised.

WORKSHOP Strategic Direction Workshop 1:
The SWOT analysis

Objective

This workshop is designed to bring together all elements of external opportunities and threats with internal strengths and weaknesses as part of management's effort to create or to refine strategic direction.

Process

1 Arrange a full-day session in a comfortable and quiet location and agree who will facilitate the process.

2 Bring together the relevant people who have the necessary knowledge, experience and insight to contribute to the session.

3 Invite anybody else who would have something useful to contribute, or if their presence or future influence is crucial for the success of the process or its implementation. Try to keep the numbers to around 12–16 participants.

4 Split the group into four sub-groups and ask them to consider a question each:
   – What are the organization's key strengths?
   – What are the organization's main weaknesses?
   – What major opportunities exist?
   – What major threats exist?

5 Give them enough time to work the process through and then ask each group to present and discuss their findings.

6 Create a large SWOT using four sheets of flip-chart paper and continue the discussion until a consensus is reached and a strategic direction emerges!

This process aims to:

• bring everyone's knowledge and insight into the analysis;

• develop agreement around the key issues;

• agree implications for the strategic direction of the organization;

• develop a consensus for the way forward.

In the author's experience, a good SWOT will tell its own story – it will clearly suggest a way forward for the organization. This is best shown by an example SWOT.

An example SWOT

A hypothetical SWOT for a UK luxury car manufacturer that might have been developed a few years ago is offered in Figure 2.5.

FIGURE 2.5 Example SWOT analysis for a luxury car manufacturer based in the UK

Strengths	*Weaknesses*
1. Strong worldwide brand	1. Lack of cash
2. World-class design and engineering resource	2. Parent company with other priorities

Opportunities	*Threats*
1. Double-digit growth in emerging markets, eg China and India	1. Zero growth in traditional markets
2. Growing affluent customer segments desiring Western brands	2. Volume manufacturers entering luxury segments

This SWOT is something the author has just put together to illustrate the point that a good SWOT suggests its own direction. If we follow the advice in the text we should now look to:

- mitigate the impact of organizational weaknesses;
- protect the organization against external threats.

But more importantly:

- exploit external opportunities with organizational strengths.

As a result of this analysis, perhaps this organization should get itself a new owner and design some of its cars for the emerging markets?

CASE STUDY   Strategic Direction Case Study 1: Mobile
phone manufacturer – From global strategy to country strategy

Background

This company is a global player in the mobile phone manufacturing industry and operates in every country around the world. The company wanted to ensure that its global strategy was effectively communicated to its various international subsidiaries around the world to enable appropriate local adaptation and implementation of the strategy.

Activity

A series of workshops were conducted in various locations around the world with those responsible for developing and implementing local sales and marketing strategy. The first part of the workshop was used to explain how the global strategy was developed, together with its key objectives. The second part of the workshop then focused on how the key global themes could be adapted to meet local market conditions to ensure effective implementation.

Key learning points

A global strategy could be effective in all national markets provided that it was explained and discussed in detail and a degree of local adaptation was permitted in order to respond to local market conditions:

- Not all aspects of the organization's global strategy were understood and the workshop cleared up any misunderstandings.

- The key global branding strategy and principal marketing messages were relevant to all markets.

- Each national market had different competitors, market structure, market growth rates and customer groupings, requiring variations in strategy.

- Each national marketing organization had a slightly different structure and people with different skills, which required variations in strategy implementation.

CASE STUDY   Strategic Direction Case Study 2: Provider
of market intelligence – Translating brand values into strategy

Background

The company provides a market intelligence and media scanning service to its clients. The company wanted to translate the work it had done on re-branding the business and identifying its key values into new ways of working and meeting the expectations of clients.

Activity

A senior management workshop was first conducted to translate the company's brand values into what clients should experience at every touch-point with the organization. These client experiences then informed the various actions and activities that needed to be delivered by the organization as a whole. Further workshops were then conducted to define the sales and service roles needed to deliver the client experiences, together with the necessary structure, management processes and reward systems required to implement the business strategy and client experience.

Key learning points

- The easy part of this process was developing the key brand values; the harder part was translating them into reality within the organization.

- Management had to work hard to identify what the brand values meant to every level in the organization, particularly how they should drive behaviour.

- A new Organizational Blueprint had to be designed to identify all customer touch-points in the organization and to develop the ideal customer experience at each point.

- It was clear that before this process many areas of the organization had very little appreciation of how other areas actually contributed to the customer experience.

- Management had to change their management style and reward structures to encourage new activities and behaviours.

CASE STUDY Strategic Direction Case Study 3: Manufacturer of swimming pools and spas – Identifying core competencies, market definition and competitive positioning

Background

The company provides swimming pools and the necessary physical infrastructure for all the wet areas and treatment areas of spas. The company wanted to identify its core competencies and its principal markets and customers.

Activity

A workshop was conducted consisting of all the senior management of the organization, together with the business heads representing the various product areas and different geographical areas of operation of the business. The workshop was split into two sub-groups and each was given a particular task.

The first group was asked to list all the areas where it thought the organization enjoyed a *core* or *distinctive competence*. The second group was asked to consider *market definition* – which markets and customers existed for the organization's product – and to recommend which ones it thought the organization should service.

Having deliberated on their specific issues, each group then presented its findings to the other, after which a debate ensued and a consensus was reached. Having reached a consensus on core competencies and market definition, the whole workshop was then asked to consider the third task: to identify the organization's desired *competitive positioning* in each of its chosen market areas.

Key learning points

- This workshop was considered vital in engaging the key players in the organization on some of the most fundamental issues that it faced and in achieving a level of consensus about their relative importance.

- This consensus was vital to enable further agreement on the preferred way forward.

- The principle of bringing key players together at regular intervals to discuss strategic issues facing the organization was well accepted and considered highly valuable.

03 Customer strategy
Who are our most important customers?

FIGURE 3.1 The Business Performance Value Chain: Customer strategy

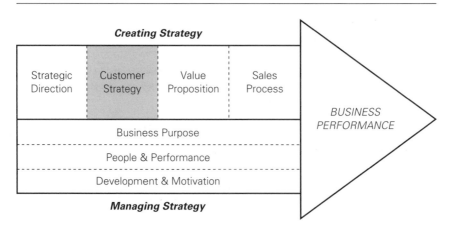

So far we have developed a strategic vision that looks to create a specific position for the organization in its chosen marketplace. This work has provided the essential foundation for all subsequent chapters in Part Two and has paved the way for our consideration of customer strategy, value proposition and sales process.

In customer strategy, we are ultimately concerned with identifying the kind of customers we want to do business with and the specific relationships we want to develop with them. In order to arrive at this destination we need to consider a number of related topics.

We will start by looking at relationship marketing and lifetime value in order to identify the contributions they make to customer strategy. We will then go on to develop a deeper understanding of customers, particularly the nature of the relationship we should develop with different categories of customer. This understanding will lead to more effective customer selection and targeting.

This chapter will also introduce the *customer journey* framework, which will help us to understand how our most important customers make buying decisions and how this knowledge will ultimately be used to develop our sales process for different categories of customer. Finally in this chapter, we will develop *customer profiles* for our target customers.

Customer strategy and marketing theory

Sales and customer strategy owes much to marketing theory. In this section we will explore the impact that two specific elements of marketing theory, namely *customer lifetime value* and *relationship marketing*, have on customer strategy.

Customer lifetime value

The theory of *customer lifetime value* is very simple. It states that the longer a customer remains a customer, the better for the organization. This is because the longer the organization keeps a customer, the more business they are going to put its way, the more revenue it will receive and, hopefully, the more profit it will make.

Figure 3.2 illustrates how customer lifetime value works.

The vertical axis measures profit and the horizontal axis measures time in years. What the diagram illustrates is that profit grows in response to the number of years a customer is retained.

The diagram also illustrates the important point that customer acquisition is expensive and often results in a negative profit (loss) in the first year following customer acquisition. This is due to the typical costs associated with winning new customers, such as introductory discounts, prolonged sales activity and the organizational learning and customer set-up costs that are incurred until normal standards of customer service delivery have been achieved.

Figure 3.2 shows the ideal case where over the lifetime of the customer relationship, increases in sales volume are enjoyed. This happens either because the customer is buying more of the same product or they are buying

FIGURE 3.2 Customer lifetime value

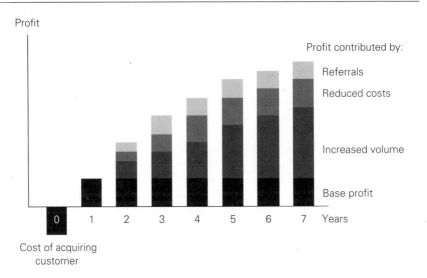

additional products. These effects are normally referred to as cross-selling and up-selling in marketing speak and they can only happen if customers are retained over the longer run.

What is also illustrated in Figure 3.2 is that the costs of servicing a customer can fall over time. This happens as the selling organization becomes more efficient at providing the product or service – the so-called learning effect.

A further feature of this diagram is the importance of customer referrals in overall profitability. The longer a customer is retained, the more likely they are to recommend the organization to others, as their loyalty must have been won through their satisfaction with the overall experience they have so far enjoyed.

There is therefore a strong incentive for organizations to retain their customers over the longer term in order to increase profits from this relationship and also to encourage referrals to potential new customers. This has important implications for customer satisfaction and loyalty and has proven the business case for ensuring that customers remain satisfied and are retained over a longer run.

Relationship marketing

The idea of relationship marketing reflects the previous discussion on customer lifetime value by suggesting that whereas the emphasis used to be on finding and winning new customers (*customer catching*), it should now shift towards developing customer relationships (*customer keeping*).

FIGURE 3.3   Relationship marketing

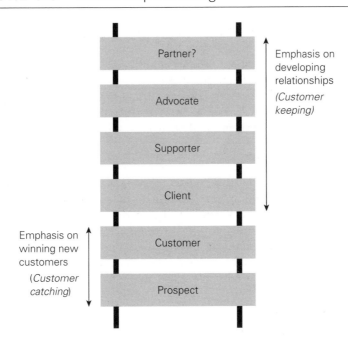

Figure 3.3 introduces the notion of the *relationship ladder*, which suggests that by altering the nature of their relationships with customers, organizations can achieve significant business benefits.

Prospect to customer

This is the traditional area of *customer catching*, where the emphasis of marketing activity is primarily on turning *prospects* into *customers*. This emphasis on winning new customers implies that once a customer has been won, the focus immediately shifts to the winning of another and then to the winning of another, and so on. The limitation of this approach is that too much emphasis is given to the winning of new customers and not enough to the development of the customer relationship. This lack of customer attention could not only lead to opportunities for further business being lost, but could in the worst case lead to customers being tempted by competitive offerings.

A customer strategy that concentrates on winning new customers without paying sufficient attention to keeping them is like trying to fill a bucket with water that has a hole in the bottom. Although winning new customers will always be an essential marketing activity, it is suggested that this should not be the single focus of any sales and customer strategy. It should also be about trying to enhance the relationship with customers in order to move them up the relationship ladder and increase business with them as a result.

Customer to client

The movement of the relationship from *customer* to *client* reflects the situation where a customer has developed from their initial position of new customer to a situation where they are now making further purchases or have started to buy additional products and services. In effect, the customer has moved from a one-off purchaser to the level of repeat customer. This reflects the notion of *customer lifetime value*, with the deepening of the customer relationship over time and the increasing levels of business being produced as a result of this mutually beneficial relationship.

Client to supporter

The movement from *client* to *supporter* reflects the increasing satisfaction of the customer with the selling organization, to the point where the customer has become an enthusiastic supporter of everything the selling organization does. In effect, the overall *customer experience* has been very positive. Customer loyalty has therefore increased to the point where customers would not normally consider moving their business elsewhere and it would therefore take a very considerable effort for any competitor to upset this relationship.

Supporter to advocate

The next movement up the relationship ladder is from *supporter* to *advocate*. At this level, not only has the customer become an enthusiastic supporter, but they are prepared to communicate their positive experience to other potential customers.

As it is often said that the best advertising comes from the recommendations of existing customers, the reaching of this stage is a very positive development in the customer relationship. Many organizations are well aware of the importance of having customers at this level of the relationship and have specific programmes designed to identify such customers and to encourage them to recruit additional customers. Adding a small financial incentive to encourage existing customers to spread the word is a very powerful sales strategy.

Advocate to partner

Moving the relationship to the next level moves an *advocate* to a *partner*. A partner relationship is a partnership of equals and implies a close collaborative relationship for mutual benefit.

With such a relationship, it is almost inconceivable that a customer will be lost to competition, as the buyer–seller relationship is so entwined. This is a specific category of relationship that we will explore further later in the chapter.

In conclusion, the notion of *relationship marketing* suggests that when looking for additional business, an organization should look first to its existing customers and strengthen its relationships with them. These relationships are the ones most likely to result in additional business in the short to medium term.

The rationale for this approach is that it should be easier to grow business with customers who already know the organization, rather than to chase new business from customers who don't. This is not to say that the organization shouldn't go after new customers, but perhaps it should think about its existing customers first.

Note: An organization might not want to enhance the relationship with all its customers in this way and, equally, not all customers would want to be so elevated.

Customer share v market share

Traditional market share is a measure of how much of the available business is held by a particular organization in a given marketplace. This is certainly a worthwhile measure of performance, but in recent years another measure has become equally important, one that is in line with what we have been talking about in relationship marketing. This measure is called *customer share*, which is more concerned with the share we have of a specific customer's business than with the share of the total market.

Figure 3.4 illustrates both customer share and market share.

FIGURE 3.4 Customer share and market share

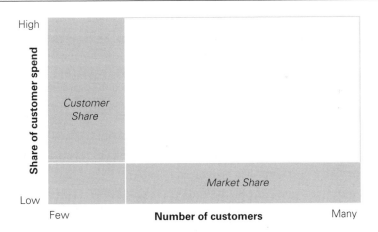

Market share is represented in this case by an organization having a small share of many customers' business, whereas customer share is represented by an organization having a high share of a few customers' business. Although measured in two different ways, the amount of total business enjoyed by both organizations could be the same (the customer share and market share blocks are a different shape, but both occupy the same total volume).

The notion of customer share, or *share of wallet*, reflects the earlier discussion in relationship marketing by suggesting that organizations should consider deepening their relationships with specific customers rather than stretching their relationship across many customers. Such a strategy implies a more focused approach to customer targeting and customer management, which allows the selling organization to better match its product and service offering to the requirements and expectations of specific customers.

The implications of marketing theory for sales and customer strategy, particularly the winning and keeping of customers, are profound. It stresses the essential link that can be traced through customer satisfaction, customer loyalty and customer retention and the impact on business performance.

This fundamental formula for business success should convince all organizations to regard existing customers as probably their most important assets and to treat them accordingly. All organizations can now develop the perfect business case to justify any initiative or strategy that seeks to improve the customer experience and thereby increase customer satisfaction and loyalty. Those organizations that have always viewed the service of customers as an unnecessary cost to be reduced wherever possible may well have to think again.

Customer importance

If he had written about customer strategy rather than about farmyard animals in the book *Animal Farm*, George Orwell might have said, '*All customers are equal, but some are more equal than others*'.

Perhaps the most fundamental aspect of customer strategy is to decide which customers are the most important and what kind of relationship the organization wants to develop with them. The status of the current customers must therefore be reviewed in order to answer these fundamental questions, as the answers will ultimately determine how scarce sales resources should be allocated to best effect.

An analysis of most organizations' customers usually reveals the following:

- A small number of customers provide most of the current business, whereas a large number provide very little.
- Some have significant further potential and will be very responsive to the organization's proposition, whereas others will not.
- Some are more at risk to competitors, whereas others are less so.
- Some are sucking in too much of the sales and service resource, whereas others are not getting enough.

Note: An organization's proposition is effectively its product and service offering. This is fully explained in Chapter 4.

These issues suggest that an organization must be able to categorize its customers and focus on those most likely to deliver good business now and in the future. Therefore a robust but simple technique to help sort out the customer priorities is needed, otherwise the organization will fail to make the most of the business opportunities offered by its various customers.

Customer understanding

Most categorizations of customer importance have been based almost exclusively on historical revenue, but this simple criterion is not sophisticated enough to provide all the information needed to make informed decisions on where to allocate sales and service resources. A robust process to generate an understanding of customers is therefore the essential starting point for any customer strategy and must address the following issues:

1 *What kind of customers does the organization have?*
2 *What type of relationship should it have with them?*
3 *Which customers (and prospects) are the most important and valuable?*
4 *How do these customers make buying decisions?*
5 *Can the organization accurately describe its ideal customers and best prospects?*

Let's look at the first two questions:

1 *What kind of customers does the organization have?*
2 *What type of relationship should it have with them?*

Some customers require almost continuous attention from various areas of the business, whereas others require very little attention even though they may generate equal amounts of business. An organization therefore needs to ensure that its customer relationships are appropriate to the requirements of different customers.

The Customer Relationship Matrix

The *Customer Relationship Matrix* is a framework that looks to identify the different types of customer and the relationship they require by evaluating them on two important points.

First, the matrix identifies the strategic or cost impact of the purchase decision from the customer's point of view. Some purchase decisions have significant commercial implications for the buying organization, either because the future of their business may depend upon getting the decision right (eg a billing system for a mobile phone operator) or because the decision has significant cost implications (eg a replacement fleet of trucks for a large haulier).

Secondly, the Customer Relationship Matrix identifies the complexity or uniqueness of the proposition from the seller's point of view. Some products and services are so complex or unique that they need a very sophisticated means of communicating them to customers and an equally sophisticated sales process for delivering this message (eg financial consultancy). Other propositions are so simple that they require very little explanation or communication (eg commodities).

The overall evaluation is represented in Figure 3.5.

FIGURE 3.5   Customer Relationship Matrix

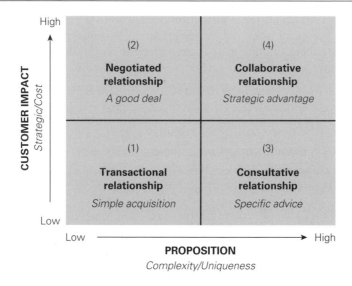

This evaluation identifies four types of relationship, as outlined below.

Type 1: Transactional relationships

Type 1 relationships are suggested when the product or service in question has a low strategic impact on the buying organization or its cost impact is relatively low. Additionally, the product or service itself is relatively un-sophisticated with little complexity or uniqueness.

Customers in this category generally require a *transactional relationship*. They require nothing more than a simple trading relationship with the supplying organization to enable them to acquire the products and services in question quickly and easily at minimum cost.

An example of this type of product would be the purchase of photocopier paper. In this kind of relationship every means of transactional efficiency should be explored, such as online or telephone ordering. Trying to add value to this kind of relationship runs the risk of merely adding unnecessary cost and complexity that has no value to the buyer and gives no benefit to the seller.

Type 2: Negotiated relationships

Type 2 relationships are suggested when the product or service purchased is very important or fundamental to the buyer's business in terms of its strategic importance or its cost impact, whereas the product or service itself is reasonably straightforward with little complexity or uniqueness.

Customers in this category require a *negotiated relationship*, as they will only buy after prolonged and serious negotiations, often taking several months and often with a number of potential suppliers. They will seek to win the best possible deal and will be prepared to change suppliers on the basis of these financial negotiations, as any small advantage they obtain in price or in trading terms can have a large impact on their business.

An example of this type of product would be the purchase of heavy trucks by a haulier or a supermarket chain as part of its national distribution system. Trucks themselves are not particularly sophisticated, but they are a very important part of the customer's business and are high-cost purchases.

From the sales organization's point of view, the need is for highly commercial salespeople with sharp financial awareness in order to negotiate win-win deals to secure the business.

Type 3: Consultative relationships

Type 3 relationships are suggested when the product or service is relatively complex or unique and therefore needs a significant amount of tailoring to meet specific customer requirements, whereas the product itself may only have a relatively minor strategic or cost impact on the buyer.

Customers in this category require a *consultative relationship*, as they require a specific variation of the product or service designed to meet their particular requirements, which can only be provided effectively on a face-to-face basis. An example of this product or service would be the provision of professional services such as accountancy advice.

From the supplying organization's point of view, the need is for technically trained professionals able to liaise with customers to understand their specific requirements, and with the ability to tailor the product or service to meet these requirements.

Type 4: Collaborative relationships

Type 4 relationships are suggested when the product or service has a high degree of complexity or uniqueness and where the strategic or cost impact of this product or service on the buyer is high. An example of this situation would be the sales of aero-engines to aircraft manufacturers.

Customers in this category require a *collaborative relationship*, as they have very particular and important requirements that demand high levels of technical and commercial cooperation. These requirements can only be fulfilled through a close and continuous relationship with the selling organization that ensures their strategic or cost objectives are met.

From the selling organization's point of view, the need here is for highly professional personnel who have the status within their own organization to marshal the required resources, and the credibility with the customer to work with them on these high-level activities. This situation might suggest the formation of an account team.

The above analysis often has an enormous impact, as organizations fully realize (often for the first time) the true nature of the various relationships implied by their different categories of customer. Although it is possible that organizations find they only have customers in one box in the Matrix, it is more usual for them to find they have a spread of customers in all four boxes. This implies the need to develop different types of relationship for different categories of customer. Some customers might require a simple, no-frills, self-service type of relationship, whereas a more strategic key account operation might be needed for others.

The above analysis leads on to the next question:

Which customers (and prospects) are the most important and valuable?

The work already done will have given some good answers to this question, although there is one refinement that might need to be addressed. We might need to look at the customers and potential customers that were placed in each of the four boxes in the Customer Relationship Matrix and decide whether they are all of equal importance or whether sales resources should be focused on some of them in particular. The answer to this question might be clear just by looking at how the customers cluster across the four boxes, but it is possible that a further analysis may be required.

Customer importance mapping

The technique of *customer importance mapping* illustrated in Figure 3.6 allows an evaluation of the customers in each of the four boxes in the Customer Relationship Matrix, in order to decide which customers (and prospects) within each of the four categories are the most important.

The vertical dimension of the map looks at customer and prospect attractiveness, which can be defined in a number of ways as outlined below.

Level of business/profitability/cash flow

Some customers have more business available than others or offer the potential for greater levels of profit. These criteria have always been a vital part of customer importance and such customers will attract interest from most suppliers in their marketplace. Other customers might provide good cash flow, which could be important to some sellers where trading conditions are difficult and credit is hard to obtain.

Loyalty

Some customers are fairly loyal in that they stay with their suppliers for a long period of time, whereas others seem to chop and change their suppliers on a regular basis. This loyalty or lack of it might be an important factor in customer attractiveness and could lead to some selling organizations targeting these customers.

Cultural fit

There are some customers that just seem to be a better fit with the selling organization than others. They can be described as *typical customers* and seem to exhibit common characteristics that can be readily recognized.

This might be due to a number of different factors, including their size, their attitude to risk, the way they like to conduct business, the elements they consider important in the buying decision, the type of individual they employ, their positioning in their own market, and the types of customer they themselves deal with. In any event, these characteristics seem to differentiate these customers from others and make them more likely to respond to the selling organization's particular proposition.

Strategic importance/industry leadership

These customers may not necessarily offer large amounts of business, but simply having them as a customer conveys a more elevated status to the selling organization. These customers or prospects have particular strategic importance, which might be due to their reputation in the industry or to the fact that all other players in that industry or market seem to take their lead from this particular organization.

When developers are planning a new shopping mall and looking to sell the space, one of the first questions other potential tenants have is whether Marks & Spencer and John Lewis are involved. Interestingly, these organizations will then be positioned at either end of the mall to stimulate customer traffic.

The horizontal dimension of the map in Figure 3.6 looks at the organization's current share of the customer's business or its relative competitive strength against those customer attractiveness factors. In this example, customers in Box A would represent the *key accounts*, as these customers are highly attractive and typically generate high levels of business. Additionally, the current position with these customers is strong and the organization enjoys a high share of this business. Customers in Box A therefore represent an organization's most important customers, as they provide most of the existing business.

The downside is that these customers will also be extremely attractive to competitors, who will be constantly targeting them with competitive offers.

FIGURE 3.6   Customer importance mapping for each type of customer

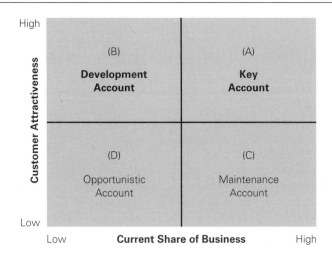

The organization must therefore focus its attention on these customers, and the best way of achieving this is via *key account planning*. This is something we will pick up in Chapter 5 on the sales process.

Customers in Box B represent the *development accounts*, as they score highly on the customer attractiveness measures outlined above but unfortunately only provide the organization with a relatively small share of this attractive business. As with key accounts, these customers require specific focus and attention as they probably represent the best source of potential new business. As such, these customers should probably be subject to account planning in the same way as key accounts.

Customers in Box C are *maintenance accounts*. These customers do not generate much attractive business, although the organization does pick up most of what does exist, which it should try to maintain.

From a strictly commercial point of view, these customers should only be provided with sufficient attention to keep their business. Typically, however, they have often enjoyed a long-term relationship with the seller and have developed solid personal relationships across the business. Such customers can therefore receive disproportionate attention, particularly from salespeople, who view these customers as a *safe call* and a reliable source of coffee.

Finally, customers in Box D are *opportunistic accounts*, as they generate little in the way of attractive business and what business they do create tends to go elsewhere. Although the organization would typically not target these customers, if they were to offer their business to it, the organization would of course oblige.

The two-stage analysis that has now been completed utilizing the Customer Relationship Matrix and Customer Importance Mapping should have provided answers to the important questions asked at the start of this section, namely: *What kind of customers does the organization have? What type of relationship should it have with them? Which customers are the most important?*

The organization should now be able to identify its most important customers and key targets, together with the appropriate relationship that these customers would require. Such decisions will have major implications for all aspects of the sales process, which we will consider in Chapter 5.

We can now turn to the next question that we posed at the beginning of this chapter:

How do these customers make buying decisions?

Customer buying decisions are very specific to each customer and no two customers make decisions in exactly the same way. However, the good news is that there are some common or generic stages in the buying process that all customers seem to go through. These are described below.

The customer journey

The *customer journey* framework represents the generic buying process and identifies the various stages in a typical customer buying experience (see Figure 3.7) . An understanding of this framework will provide some important insights into those factors that are important to customers and how they make buying decisions. An organization can then use this framework to identify what is important to its own particular customers and how *they* make buying decisions.

FIGURE 3.7   The customer journey (buying process)

Customer Journey	Need	Search	Evaluation	Decision	Review
	Having a Requirement	*Looking for Help*	*Examining the Options*	*Making a Commitment*	*Evaluating Experience*
What happens? (DMP)					
What's important? (Key Purchase Criteria)					
Who's involved? (DMU)					

The typical customer journey (customer buying process) consists of five key stages as follows:

NEED – SEARCH – EVALUATION – DECISION – REVIEW

It is possible that the four different categories of customer identified in the Customer Relationship Matrix may have totally different buying processes and it may therefore be necessary to identify the specific customer journey for each different category of customer.

During each of these five stages of the customer journey, the seller is seeking to understand:

- *What happens?* The particular stages in the *decision making process (DMP)* for the customer in question and the relative timescales for each stage.
- *What's important?* The basis of how any decisions are made at any point in this buying process, particularly how a need arises, how a search for information is made, how purchase options are evaluated, what is important in the buying decision, and how purchase decisions are subsequently reviewed.
- *Who's involved?* The involvement of various individuals in the *decision-making unit (DMU)*, together with their importance.

We will explore the dynamics of the DMU in more detail in Chapter 5 on the sales process, and how this DMU can be managed as part of account strategy. Going back to the customer journey framework:

Customers start with a *NEED*.

Customers have a need in response to something that is happening in any area of the business. This need could be to move away from a negative condition or a negative situation such as high costs. Alternatively, this requirement could be to move towards a positive situation, such as an aspiration to move into a specific product area or marketplace.

Either way, this requirement will provide a need in the buying organization that the seller can exploit. However, at this early stage in the buying process the need is not fully understood and therefore the customer is not able to fully articulate the nature of their specific requirement. This lack of clarity provides an opportunity for the seller to help the buyer fully understand the nature of their requirement.

An important implication for the seller is therefore that they should try to identify those organizations that are at this early stage of their buying process. The earlier the seller can get involved, the more likely they are to be able to influence the buying process. (When we look at the sales process in Chapter 5, all the implications of the customer journey for the seller will be examined.)

The next stage in the customer journey is a *SEARCH*.

During this stage, customers look around for something or someone who can help them with their requirements. This search process may be informal, consisting of a quick search of potential suppliers, or a very formal process with many separate aspects. This search process can therefore include tendering, beauty parades of potential suppliers, internet searches, searches through trade journals or the trade press, visits to trade fairs or exhibitions, responses to advertising or promotions, or asking other companies for recommended suppliers.

The potential ways that customers can search is seemingly daunting, but customers in specific industries often have preferred sources of information, which the seller needs to identify. As far as the seller is concerned, they can of course be in the right place at the right time when the customer makes the search, but more realistically, the seller should try to identify the most appropriate information channels for their specific customer group and ensure they are adequately represented in these channels.

The next stage in the customer journey is an *EVALUATION*.

Customers have by now come to the end of their review stage and may well have gathered a significant amount of information relating to potential suppliers and their products. Therefore, a number of different purchase options may now exist that could potentially meet their requirements.

Customers now have to evaluate these options to decide upon the one that comes closest to meeting their specific requirements. Customers in B2B markets often have some formalized *key purchase criteria* that form the basis of this evaluation that are used to rate the various options available to them.

Key purchase criteria typically include price, performance, delivery and any other elements important to the buying organization. A major objective for any selling organization is therefore to identify what these purchase criteria are in order to communicate their product and service offering in the most powerful way. It may even be possible for the selling organization to influence what criteria the buying organization chooses to use to evaluate their options, if it can become involved at the early stages of the customer buying process before the nature of the requirement has been fully determined.

A further aim is to identify who within the buying organization is involved in this evaluation of the various purchase options, and the specific roles they take in this process. The constitution of a typical decision-making unit (DMU) is something we will explore in detail in Chapter 5 on the sales process.

The next stage in the customer journey is the *DECISION*.

At this stage, customers reach a buying decision. They make a choice as a result of the evaluation they have made.

Although buyers always claim to make rational and informed choices by comparing their purchase criteria against the rival product and service offerings, in reality these choices are often made on subjective and non-rational criteria. Those making formal buying decisions can still be swayed by such things as intuition and gut-feel, including whether or not they like the seller and the selling organization.

A further complication is that in large organizations, the decision-making process can be quite involved. It can take a long time and involve many different individuals with their own particular agendas.

In response, the selling organization needs a professional sales activity in order to press its case for selection during this crucial stage in the buying process. We will explore the need for specific sales skills at each stage of the customer buying process in the chapters on sales process (Chapter 5) and people and performance (Chapter 7).

The final stage of the customer journey is a *REVIEW*.
Most major purchase decisions are subject to review; that is, they are re-examined at some later stage in light of the actual experience of working with the selling organization or of using the product or service in question. The review considers whether the purchase decision was the right one and ensures that the product or service purchased did in fact deliver what it was supposed to deliver. The review is usually made against the original specification or against the key performance indicators or service level agreements made at the time of purchase.

This stage in the buying process is often overlooked by the seller. However, it is a crucial requirement for the continuation of a successful business relationship and for possible further business.

This whole process from *need* to *review* can take only a few minutes, for example in the case of buying a bar of chocolate while queuing to pay for petrol, but even this purchase will follow the generic buying process:

- NEED – *I fancy a snack.*
- SEARCH – *What's on the shelf by the counter?*
- EVALUATION – *I fancy chocolate rather than anything else.*
- DECISION – *I'll buy the Twix rather than the Snickers.*
- REVIEW – *Mmm, that did the job.*

Typical B2B buying decisions are obviously much more complicated in terms of time, money and people involved. Therefore, a key element of sales and customer strategy is to understand the buying decisions of the different types of target customers.

Sources of customer information

There are a number of important sources of information that allow an organization to develop an understanding of its customers and how they make buying decisions.

Published sources

Organizations like to talk about their own achievements and plans, particularly to their investors. As a result there is usually a considerable amount of customer information that can be found in published sources, including their own financial statements and their own PR material. Newspapers and trade journals are other important sources where specific announcements and comments from key individuals can often provide important insights into the buying organization.

Market research

There are often market research studies available on particular industries that will provide insights into how customers in those industries behave. There may even be research reports that exist for specific customers that are actual targets of the selling organization. These reports may provide very detailed information about these customers' strategies, plans and what they look for from their supplier relationships.

Fellow suppliers

Other non-competing suppliers are a good source of customer information, as these organizations will have faced similar issues of getting to know the buying organization and may be willing to share their knowledge.

Former employees

We are not about to slip into commercial espionage at this point, but former employees of the buying organization who now work for the selling organization can quite legitimately provide valuable information about how their former employers make buying decisions, what is important in these decisions, and who is involved in the process.

However, in the final analysis there is no substitute for making initial contact with the organization and then networking your way around it to slowly build up knowledge of the customer until an adequate understanding is achieved. This particular aspect of intelligence gathering will be fully explored in Chapter 5 on the sales process.

So now to the final question in this chapter:

Can the organization accurately describe its ideal customers and best prospects?

Customer profiling

A useful exercise to bring customer understanding into sharp focus is developing *customer profiles* for each type of customer. These profiles may reflect

the specific categories of customer identified using the Customer Relationship Matrix explored earlier, and will represent a short summary of a typical customer in that particular customer group or category.

Figure 3.8 illustrates the key elements in any customer profile.

FIGURE 3.8   Customer profiling

Customer category and description

This reflects the work done on customer importance by identifying the important categories of customer, together with a brief description.

Key requirements

This reflects the work done in understanding customers, particularly in identifying the key purchase criteria that define what they regard as crucial in any buying decision.

Buying process

This element reflects how this category of customer makes buying decisions. In particular, it identifies the specific stages that this category of customer passes through, from their initial identification of a need to how they review any subsequent buying decision. The customer profile also identifies who is typically involved in a buying decision and their relative importance at every stage in the buying process.

Relationship required

This reflects the work done to identify what kind of relationship is appropriate for this category of customer. This relationship can range from a *transactional relationship* with customers that only want to acquire the product and service in the simplest and most cost-effective way, through to customers that require a *collaborative relationship* that might involve many areas of the organization providing an input to this relationship.

The acid test of a good customer profile is whether it creates a clear picture of the type of customer being targeted in the mind's eye, purely by reading the description. An effective customer profile can also stimulate consideration of how such customers can be best approached to communicate the value of the organization's product and service offering.

In other words, a segmentation model has been produced that defines those customers and prospects that provide the best opportunity for business. These customer profiles will be a very important reference point for all aspects of the sales and customer strategy, as they represent those customers that it is most important to *win* and *keep*.

Previewing sales process

If an organization has identified the typical journey of its own customers accurately, it can then identify the specific moments of truth or tipping points that occur when customers move through their buying process. These moments of truth need to be influenced by the selling organization to ensure the customer arrives at the right destination.

This customer understanding will form the basis of the *sales process*, which aims to influence the course of this customer journey to favour the organization's own particular product and service offering. This sales process will therefore reflect the five stages of the buying process that were previously identified.

It can be difficult to think about customers without wanting to move straight into selling mode, and we have already mentioned a number of implications for the sales process during this chapter. Therefore, as a preview of what will be discussed in Chapter 5, the following diagram (Figure 3.9) is provided for information. It outlines the topics that will be explored under *finding*, *engaging*, *proving*, *winning* and *keeping*.

FIGURE 3.9   The customer journey and sales process

	Need	Search	Evaluation	Decision	Review
Customer Journey (Buying Process)	Having a Requirement	Looking for Help	Examining the Options	Making a Commitment	Evaluating Experience
	Finding	**Engaging**	**Proving**	**Winning**	**Keeping**
Sales Process	Searching	Opening	Features / Benefits	Objection Handling	Customer Satisfaction
	Prospecting	Analysis / Fact Find	Value Proposition	Trading Value	Relationship Development
	Qualifying	Summary & Vision	References	Negotiation	Added Value

Workshops and case studies

A number of workshops and case studies can be found below, designed to help the reader apply some of the techniques discussed in the chapter and to illustrate how organizations have coped with some of the issues raised.

WORKSHOP   Customer Strategy Workshop 1:
The Customer Relationship Matrix

Objective

This workshop is designed to identify the nature of the customer relationships you have with your customers.

Process

1   Draw the Customer Relationship Matrix found on page 44 on a full page of a flip chart and label the axes and boxes as described in the text.

2   Take your full list of B2B customers and put each customer into the box that represents the type of relationship it deserves.

3   When the exercise is complete, take a look at the spread of customers across the sheet and consider what it is telling you.

Key questions

- Do you have an even spread of customers in each box or are they clustered in particular boxes?

- Is your sales organization giving each customer the appropriate relationship?

- Are you trying to be 'all things to all men'?

- Are you giving too much sales and service resource to some customers? Are you not giving enough resource to those that deserve more?

This exercise is the starting point of orientating your sales and customer strategy around the most important customers.

WORKSHOP Customer Strategy Workshop 2:
Customer Importance Mapping

Objective

This workshop will help prioritize the most important customers and prospects within each relationship category.

Process

The output from Workshop I may need to be further refined, as you might have a large number of customers in each of the four boxes that need further prioritization. Alternatively, in some cases the Customer Relationship Matrix may not be a useful tool for analysing customers in your particular situation, especially if all your customers are clustered in only one box and require the same relationship. In either case, Customer Importance Mapping will be useful.

1   Take a sheet of flip-chart paper and draw the customer importance mapping outline, labelling the axes and boxes as per the text.

2   You should decide upon your own criteria that you regard as important for *customer attractiveness*. These criteria can include:
  – level of business/profitability/cash flow;
  – loyalty;
  – cultural fit;
  – strategic importance/industry leadership.

3   Now enter the customers into the appropriate boxes in the matrix.

4   When the exercise is complete, take a look at the spread of customers across the sheet and consider what it is telling you.

Key questions

- Do you have some clear key accounts (Box A)?

- Are they managed by highly skilled key account managers?

- Do these accounts have key account plans?

- Are there some development accounts (Box B) that should also be prioritized as they provide the best opportunity for additional good business?

- Are there other accounts that fall into Boxes C and D that can be managed in a different way, using less resource?

What you are really looking for are those customers that fit in Boxes A and B, as they deliver most of your current business and provide the best opportunities for additional business. These accounts should therefore receive most of your sales and service attention and resource.

WORKSHOP   Customer Strategy Workshop 3:
The customer journey

Objective

This workshop is designed to identify how your most important customers and prospects make buying decisions. It utilizes the customer journey framework introduced in the text to structure your thinking around gaining this customer knowledge and understanding.

Process

1 Take a sheet of flip-chart paper and reproduce the customer journey framework from page 49.

2 Now select a typical example customer from your key accounts or development account list and complete the framework to answer the questions below.

Key questions

- How does a need arise? What are its triggers?

- How do they search for potential suppliers to help them?

- What purchase criteria do they use to judge competing offers?

- How do they make purchase decisions? Who is involved?

- How often do they review purchase decisions and supplier experiences?

Within your list of key accounts or development accounts you may find that there are some significant differences in the customer journeys, with certain types of customer buying in very different ways from others. The only way to check for this is to run the analysis a few times to pick up any key differences, which may suggest the existence of different customer categories that might need to be handled differently. The results of this analysis will be very important when we come to develop sales process in Chapter 5.

CASE STUDY   Customer Strategy Case Study 1:
Truck manufacturer – Creating customer profiles

Background

This international truck manufacturer wanted to understand its customers in order to better respond to their requirements and expectations. In previous workshops, the Customer

Relationship Matrix had identified that most customers required a *negotiated relationship* and the use of customer importance mapping had identified their key accounts and development accounts.

Activity

When using the customer journey methodology, three distinct customer segments emerged, each with their own specific purchase criteria and decision-making processes. This required that these segments be managed differently in terms of the sales process and account plans. Customer profiles were developed for each of these segments as follows:

1 *Owner-operators* – often family businesses owning their own trucks in their own distinct livery:

   – With owner-operators, a need could suddenly arise if a truck broke down irretrievably or if a piece of business was won requiring a different type of truck.

   – Before buying, these operators would normally consult their informal network of contacts for their views on various trucks available on the market.

   – Buying decisions were normally made fairly quickly, with perhaps only members of the family consulted.

2 *Large haulier fleets* – trucking goods long distances around the country:

   – These fleets, such as Tesco, tested a number of trucks from different manufacturers until they made a decision.

   – A number of different people were involved in the buying decision, even at board level, before a decision was made, which could take a considerable time.

3 *Local authorities* – needing to deliver local services:

   – Local authorities were very driven by budget timescales and were relatively inflexible in their replacement cycles and buying decisions.

   – Local authorities tended to talk to each other and to share information, particularly about the type of truck most suitable for various tasks, such as refuse collection.

Key learning points

- It was very difficult to identify the different ways that owner-operators, large hauliers and local authorities made buying decisions until they were all subjected to the customer journey methodology. This identified the key differences in their buying processes.

- All the necessary information to enable the development of customer profiles existed in the sales team but it had never previously been brought together.

- The various workshops developed the desire for the sales team to re-engage with their customers in a more effective way.

CASE STUDY Customer Strategy Case Study 2:
Tyre manufacturer – Identifying customer relationships

Background

A leading tyre manufacturer completed the Customer Relationship Matrix and found they were giving the same level of sales and service resource to all customers. *Transactional customers* in Box 1 were receiving personal visits from expensive salespeople, when all they really needed was a regular telephone call to re-order tyres.

On the other hand, there were a number of customers who specialized in sports tyres, offering bespoke alloy wheels and other after-market accessories. These *collaborative customers* in Box 4 required more sophisticated product and merchandising support, but they in fact only received the same level of attention as transactional customers.

The tyre manufacturer then completed the second-level analysis provided by the Customer Importance Mapping framework to identify their key accounts and development accounts.

Activity

The analysis was completed by every account manager in every sales territory and covered all the organization's customers. It was implemented as follows:

1 A telephone account management unit was set up to contact transactional customers on a regular basis to quickly and effectively replenish their stocks against an agreed tyre stocking profile.

2 This unit took a considerable number of customers off the hands of account managers and enabled them to concentrate their resources on key accounts and development accounts that required a more collaborative relationship.

3 A training programme was developed for account managers to develop their knowledge and skills so that they could provide more high-level product and marketing advice for these more important accounts.

Key learning points

- Before the analysis, most salespeople did not have a system for ensuring they spent their time in the most productive way.

- It was found that customer importance provided the best way of ensuring effective time and territory management.

- The creation of customer profiles identified a specific category of customer more responsive to the organization's proposition than other categories. These customers represented most of their development accounts.

CASE STUDY Customer Strategy Case Study 3:
Local cinema – Recruiting customer advocates (1)

Background

This local cinema is now a registered charity and has been in continuous use since it opened in 1912. The cinema had previously conducted market research to identify why customers came to the cinema and what they liked best about it.

During the course of this research, many customers made it clear that they were very proud of the cinema and would be very willing to do anything else they could to continue its success. There was clearly a very strong emotional attachment between the cinema and its customers.

The cinema wanted to capitalize on its history and its positioning in the local marketplace to attract customers to attend on a more regular basis.

Activity

The cinema recruited some of its more committed customers and those that had large social networks to become its *ambassadors*. Their role was to be kept informed of upcoming film presentations and to encourage their network of friends to come along, and to encourage others to do the same. The ambassadors were also provided with a limited amount of free tickets to reward them for their role and to use as inducements for new customers.

Key learning points

- Some customers have a very close relationship with organizations, to the point where they have in fact developed a powerful emotional connection with them.

- Some customers are delighted to demonstrate this connection by helping these organizations to develop their business and become more successful.

- What existing customers say about an organization to other customers is more powerful than any advertising or promotion.

- Providing a small incentive to these customers to spread the word can generate significant benefits.

CASE STUDY Customer Strategy Case Study 4:
Manufacturer of swimming pools – recruiting customer advocates (2)

Background

The company manufactures and supplies swimming pools to home owners in certain markets in the Arabian Gulf. The company wanted to capitalize on their growing reputation for providing 'pools for the home owner' by encouraging recent purchasers to become advocates to other prospective customers.

Activity

A programme to encourage new owners to invite family and friends to the opening of their new pool was developed. These owners were provided with the necessary food and drink for any kind of social gathering of their choice.

Key learning points

- Swimming pools are purchased for a number of reasons, but particularly for family fun, to increase the value of property, and as a backdrop for social interaction, such as a barbeque or evening party.

- Swimming pools are also status symbols that owners like to show off to their family and friends.

- New owners can be incentivized to throw 'pool parties' for friends who might well become interested in a pool of their own.

- A small incentive such as providing the new owner with everything for a barbecue can stimulate them to spread the word to their community of friends.

The value proposition
How can our products and services create unique customer value?

04

FIGURE 4.1 The Business Performance Value Chain:
Value proposition

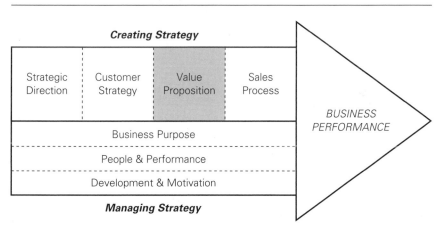

The third element of creating strategy is *the value proposition*. We will use the *Total Proposition Methodology* to identify the full extent of the product and service offering. We will also use the *Differentiator Matrix* to identify which of these elements can create positive differentiation in the mind of the customer.

We will use the *Value Mapping Methodology* to identify how customer value can be created from all aspects of the total proposition, together with the *Value Balance Sheet* to demonstrate how value can be quantified, communicated and traded to win customer commitment. Finally, we will use the *Value Proposition Creator* to create customer value propositions for typical customers.

Products and services

As election time approaches, politicians may remind themselves of the most important thing on voters' minds by remembering the phrase: *It's the economy, stupid!* In sales and marketing, there is perhaps a similar phrase that all of us should keep in mind: *It's the product, stupid!* This might seem like an obvious statement of fact, but sometimes even the most obvious stuff gets lost along the way.

At the beginning of Part Two we spent some time considering *strategic direction*, and in Part Three we will spend an equal amount of time considering the organization's *business purpose* – essential elements that support sales and customer strategy. However, in the final analysis, all of this will come to nothing if we fail to produce products and services that customers want to buy.

Coming from the automotive industry, the author knows only too well the pressure of trying to find customers for un-loved or uncompetitive products, particularly when the competition has products that customers are falling over themselves to buy. Therefore, in this section we are going to give a significant amount of attention to the products and services offered by the organization to its chosen marketplace.

The total proposition

Having discussed how important products and services are to the organization's commercial health, we are now going to introduce *the total proposition*, which stands for the combination of both. There are a couple of good reasons for this.

Firstly, in the B2B environment products are often sold with an extensive service element included in the total package, and in some cases consist entirely of a service with no physical product at all. As a result, the distinction between what is a product and what is a service becomes rather blurred.

Secondly, and most importantly, we want to examine the total extent of what the organization can offer to its customers; that is, we want to make sure that we do not overlook any element of this potential product/service mix. This will become even more important when we go on to consider *customer value* and how various elements of the total proposition can come together in different combinations to create value for a variety of different customers.

In order to reflect this situation, we will use the term *total proposition* to imply the full extent of the product and service offering that can be provided to customers.

FIGURE 4.2   The total proposition

Figure 4.2 illustrates all the elements that make up the total proposition, and can be used to identify the full extent of the organization's total product and service offering. This framework provides an excellent opportunity to re-evaluate every aspect of what the organization offers to customers and is important for those responsible for developing and delivering sales and customer strategy.

Product aspects

This element refers to the actual physical manifestation of the product or service but also includes its performance measured by speed, time saved, output created or any other aspect of measurable performance. Delivery is another aspect of product performance, both in terms of delivery lead time and also completeness and reliability of delivery. Style, design or technical specification can also represent important aspects of the total proposition, together with anything relating to its reputation.

Technical aspects

The technical aspects of the total proposition include anything related to the product's installation, such as its speed or the lack of disruption to existing operations. It also includes anything related to technology, such as provision of new technology or technology transfer. Additionally, advice provided for the product's continuous operations, including technical advice, represents a further aspect of the total proposition.

Financial aspects

The financial aspects of the total proposition can be particularly important. Such things as the terms of business, payment terms, promotions, discounts and loans can offer strong inducements for customers to place their business in a particular direction. Anything that the organization can provide in these areas of financial support could be crucial in influencing customer choice, particularly during periods of credit shortage and strains on cash flow.

Networks

This aspect relates to any particular alliances or partnerships the organization enjoys with any other organization that might be of interest to customers. These alliances and networks might provide access to particular expertise, sources of information or technical data that will add value to the organization's own products and services. Furthermore, these alliances and networks might provide access to those customers that might not be reachable otherwise, thereby creating additional business opportunities.

Image

Image, status and the overall value of the brand are important elements that impact on the customer buying decision. They are therefore potentially valuable aspects of the total proposition that can be exploited.

Customer endorsements or referrals are another important aspect of the organization's total proposition, particularly online rating systems, which are becoming increasingly influential in customer consideration and customer choice. Amazon is a particularly good example of this phenomenon. In addition to providing customer ratings of the product, they also provide recommendations for additional purchases based on the purchasing profiles of other customers with similar interests.

A further aspect of increasing importance is the organization's green credentials with regard to waste handling, recycling and carbon emissions. This can sometimes tip the balance in a sale.

Marketing aspects

One important aspect of an organization's total proposition is its customer reach; that is, the range and number of customers that it is able to engage with. This can relate to the ability to reach specific customer groups, to the organization's geographical coverage, or to its use of all the various means (physical or electronic) that customers have available when accessing the organization.

Other marketing elements, such as the power and creativity of advertising and the organization's capability in new product development, particularly its success in bringing exciting new products to market, are also key elements of its total proposition. The organization's sales force, especially its effectiveness and flexibility in coping with various market conditions, competitive actions and customer requirements, can also represent a very important aspect of the organization's total proposition in B2B markets.

Quality

Product and service quality is an important element of any organization's total proposition. It is ultimately measured by overall customer satisfaction at various points during the customer experience.

The provision of warranties and guarantees are another way that organizations can demonstrate the quality and reliability of their total proposition. The ability of customers to share their buying experiences and quality perceptions online makes this aspect of the total proposition increasingly important.

Support

This element relates to any aspect of the total proposition that adds something extra to the customer's experience. It can include the provision of consultancy advice on either product selection or product usage and can also include after-sales service.

Additionally, thought should be given to any specific *core competencies* or *organizational capabilities* that the organization enjoys. We have already considered these aspects in Chapter 2 on strategic direction, but they should be included in this section too as they will be important when we look at creating customer value.

Any of the above aspects of the total proposition could make the vital difference to a potential customer during the buying process to determine a sale or a no-sale. As competitive superiority can be decided on the smallest of margins, every possible advantage provided by the organization's total product and service proposition should be identified and documented.

New product development

The subject of new product development is an extensive subject in its own right and as such is outside the scope of this book. However, some issues relating to this important subject are worth mentioning here.

The importance of product renewal

Products and services are the lifeblood of the business, and as such they should be under continuous review. This scrutiny should not only be confined to sales volume and market share, but should also include customer perceptions of the product relative to competitors, and customer satisfaction with the whole purchase process from initial consideration through to eventual purchase choice, product use and possible re-purchase. This vital intelligence should be shared around the organization to inform the product development process and ensure that the most appropriate new products are brought to market at the right time.

Where the best ideas come from

New product ideas can come from a variety of sources, but the best ones often come from customers themselves. It is enlightening to watch customers use your product and to listen to them talk about what they find useful about it and what they don't. Additionally, their views on how the product could be improved and their thoughts on potential new products that might satisfy their needs better than existing ones are fascinating. This poses the question of who should be responsible for customer research in the first place?

Who does the research?

Most market research is undertaken by marketing research agencies that use trained professionals to complete the entire research process. This process includes the design of the research study, the recruitment of respondents, the data collection and analysis, and the writing and presenting of the final report for the client. This research process is certainly very professional, but does the outsourcing of this valuable opportunity for customer contact and understanding miss an opportunity?

As a consultant, I have often provided sales and marketing executives with the basic research skills as part of a training and development programme, and then asked them to conduct real research with real customers. These studies have always been fairly small-scale, qualitative studies, usually based around the identification of customers' key purchase criteria or testing potential new product ideas. However, in every case the impact of this research has been dramatic.

The opportunity to talk to real customers about their perceptions, requirements and expectations has often transformed the views of these amateur researchers. It has a particularly marked impact on their understanding of how customers think, how they compare alternative product offerings and how they make buying decisions. These small-scale studies, which should of course be validated by more detailed research, can often create more profound insights into the organization's competitive positioning and possible future direction than larger-scale quantitative studies, which may provide endless data but relatively few insights.

This raises a wider point about the closeness of organizations to their customers. Many have increasingly distanced themselves from their customers by hiding behind complicated organization structures or impersonal customer relationship management (CRM) systems and software. The author believes this to be a great danger, as this lack of essential contact can lead to a lack of customer understanding, and ultimately to poor sales and customer strategy.

Differentiation

Putting together the total proposition is a very useful exercise and in most cases the number of different aspects identified comes as a pleasant surprise. It is common for executives in workshop sessions to fill whole sheets of flip-chart paper with different aspects of their total proposition, some forgotten due to over-familiarity and others discovered for the first time.

However, it is not unusual to find that many aspects of the organization's total proposition are also offered by competitors. Therefore, the next stage of the analysis is to identify those aspects that provide competitive advantage, by being unique to the organization, important to customers, and difficult to copy. In other words, an organization needs to find those elements of the total proposition that will differentiate it from the competition and will hopefully lead to customers beating a path to its door.

Unique to us

Competitive advantage is based on being able to do something different from or better than competitors. In any aspect of competition, the margins between being first and being nowhere are very small. In the Olympic 100 m final, the difference between winning the gold medal and winning no medal at all is only a few tenths of a second. Similarly, in commercial competition a competitive advantage does not have to be huge, but it does have to be big enough to register in the mind of the customer.

Important to customers

Identifying a competitive advantage is important, but identifying whether it creates customer value is equally important. A competitive advantage is only valuable to the organization if it is important in the mind of the customer.

In marketing there is a phrase: *perception is reality*. It means that in the final analysis, it is what the customer thinks that is important, not what the organization believes to be true. If a customer believes that an organization has good customer service then this specific perception of reality is the only one that really matters.

A further issue is that different types of customer have different requirements and expectations; therefore, it must be decided which group of customers is being considered. An organization must have a specific group of customers in mind when it completes this analysis and should also bear in mind that different things can be important to different people.

Difficult to copy

The competitive advantage for an organization of having aspects of the proposition that are both unique and valuable to customers is made even more important if these advantages are difficult for competitors to copy. Some competitive advantages are harder for competitors to copy than others.

For example, financial advantages relating to prices, discounts and trading terms can be copied with the click of a mouse, providing the financial muscle exists to do so. Product advantages relating to the performance or specification of the product are also relatively easy to copy. The addition of a product feature today can be copied by a competitor tomorrow (or at least in a few weeks).

The advantages that are more difficult to copy are those that relate to any aspect of the total proposition where the organization has exclusive access. This may be to raw materials, technology, business processes, customers and markets, or people and skills.

The reputation of the organization and its products or its brand image are also elements of competitive advantage that are difficult to copy, as they have often been developed over time through a consistent and focused strategy. Similarly, advantages relating to any aspect of the customer experience, such as customer service and after-sales support, are equally hard for competitors to copy.

These *sustainable competitive advantages* provide the organization with more time to exploit them in winning and keeping customers and in growing the business. These advantages represent the *crown jewels* of any organization, providing the opportunity to create real competitive differentiation in the marketplace.

FIGURE 4.3   The Differentiator Matrix

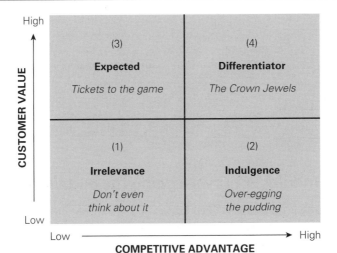

The Differentiator Matrix

The Differentiator Matrix in Figure 4.3 is a framework that allows an organization to evaluate all aspects of its total proposition in order to identify those that can provide it with competitive advantage.

This matrix takes all of those elements of the total proposition identified earlier and evaluates them using two different dimensions. The horizontal dimension looks at whether the proposition element has any competitive advantage, whereas the vertical dimension looks at the customer value of that element.

Each dimension has a simple scale: low to high. Where the reader places any particular element on this scale is therefore a matter of executive judgement. The existence of any customer research on these issues will of course make this analysis easier, but even without this information, useful judgements can still be made.

The Differentiator Matrix, like most other frameworks in this book, is *directional*. This means it is not designed to give precise answers to any question of strategy, but rather to give overall guidance and direction towards an answer that makes sense for the organization.

In this framework every element of the total proposition is transferred into the relevant box in the matrix.

Box 1 – Irrelevance (don't even think about it)

Aspects of the total proposition placed in this box are adjudged to have low competitive advantage, together with low value to the customer. Such elements of the proposition are considered to be an *irrelevance*, as they do not appear to serve any useful purpose to the organization or to customers.

These aspects of the proposition are probably what remain from previous iterations of the product or service that have either been superseded over time or have been forgotten about. The only effect that such aspects have on the proposition is to add unnecessary complexity or cost with no return on investment.

Aspects that fall into the *don't even think about it* category are prime candidates for deletion and can be removed from the total proposition without penalty. At the very least they are not things that would feature in any aspect of sales and customer strategy.

Box 2 – Indulgence (over-egging the pudding)

Aspects of the proposition placed in this box are subtly different from those in Box 1. They do at least demonstrate some aspect of competitive advantage and represent something the organization can provide better than the competition. They are nevertheless an *indulgence*. This is due to the chosen customers regarding such advantages as having no value, and as such these aspects of the total proposition will not cause customers to beat a path to the organization's door any time soon.

Such aspects can be said to be *over-egging the pudding* because they again create complexity or cost without creating anything of value to the customer. They are certainly not aspects that would feature in any sales and customer strategy and could be quietly deleted altogether.

Box 3 – Expected (taken for granted)

Those aspects of the total proposition in Box 3 demonstrate high value to customers, or at least represent aspects that are *expected* by customers as part of any product or service offering. However, as these aspects are expected and taken for granted by customers, all organizations in this marketplace are obliged to provide them as part of their total proposition, even though they create no competitive advantage whatsoever.

Such elements are therefore merely *tickets to the game*. They ensure that the organizations providing them are at least considered to be legitimate players in the marketplace so that customers do not go elsewhere. All these *expected* elements of the total proposition must thus be featured in any sales and customer communications to provide reassuring signals to customers.

Box 4 – Differentiator (the crown jewels)

Attributes of the total proposition that fall into Box 4 are the 'holy grail' of sales and customer strategy that we referred to earlier. Such aspects represent the ideal combination of being both valuable to customers and unique to the organization. They therefore represent the organization's *crown jewels*.

These are the things that customers will come to know the organization for, and the things that will create clear blue water between the organization and its competition. They are the aspects of the total proposition that will feature most strongly in those aspects of the sales and customer strategy that communicate how the organization will create value for its customers. They are the elements around which the organization can build a sustainable competitive position for itself.

When completing the analysis using the Differentiator Matrix, it is not unusual to see aspects of the total proposition in all four boxes. The good news, however, is that never in the author's experience has any organization failed to identify any good candidates for Box 4. This means that every organization has its own crown jewels. The key question then becomes: *How do we get the biggest bang from the buck?* That is, how do organizations exploit these key differentiators to maximum effect?

Creating customer value

From the work in the last section, all aspects of the total proposition have now been identified. In particular, some elements have been identified that will help to differentiate the organization from the competition.

It is very important that we don't waste this effort by going no further in the exploration of what this particular aspect of the proposition can deliver to the customer. We therefore have a further stage to go through before we have finished with this section; we need to consider the whole question of *customer value*.

Customer value is measured by what a product or service allows a customer to do. Another way of saying this is that customers do not buy what something is, they buy what it does. This is particularly true when selling services to business customers, where the nature of these services can often be intangible.

We therefore need to translate the proposition elements into customer value and to communicate this in the most effective way possible. In order to understand what value is, we need to take a little sales skills refresher. We need to explore the difference between three important concepts: *features*, *benefits* and *value*.

Features

A feature is purely a description of some aspect of the product or service identified under the total proposition framework above. This description provides no further information other than this basic definition.

An example of a product feature is an automatic gearbox on a car. This description identifies the product feature pretty well, mainly because it is a well-known feature that most of us have had the experience of. A problem arises when the product feature is not well known and therefore the description tells you absolutely nothing about what the product is or what it does. Even when the feature is well understood, this mere description of some aspect of the product or service does not go far enough; it still does not communicate to the customer what this feature will do for them.

One of the basic problems in sales is the over-use of features when communicating products and services to customers. Merely throwing a list of product features at a customer is not going to fill them with enthusiasm for the product. That dreadful malaise, *death by feature*, is something that many salespeople (and customers) suffer from. We therefore need to avoid this problem by exploring what product and service features can do for the customer.

Benefits

A *benefit* is some advantage that the proposition or some feature of it can produce for a customer. Most product and service features can produce benefits of some kind or other, although it is not unusual to find that some product features have no discernible benefits at all.

Value

Value is the measurable advantage that a specific benefit can bring to a specific customer. Some benefits can therefore be of no value to a customer. The challenge for salespeople is to translate potential benefits into value that the customer can understand and appreciate.

In summary:

- Feature – One aspect of the proposition
- Benefit – Potential advantage offered by the feature
- Value – Value of that benefit for a specific customer

Let's look at some examples.

Example 1

- Feature – Automatic gearbox
- Benefit – Easier driving
- Value – To an older driver with arthritis: considerable. To a young boy racer: zero.

Example 2

- Feature – Better credit terms
- Benefit – More cash in the business
- Value – To a business with tight cash flow: survival. To a cash-rich business: little value.

Example 3

- Feature – Faster machine
- Benefit – More output
- Value – Increased revenue/reduction in costs

Example 4

- Feature – Consultancy advice
- Benefit – Identification of business opportunities
- Value – To all businesses: considerable!

What becomes clear is that value is something that is specific to a particular customer. What is valuable to one customer may not be valuable to another.

Furthermore, a particular feature can produce a number of benefits, only one of which might create value for a specific customer, whereas the same benefit could create a completely different value for another. The ultimate objective is of course to win the sale by persuading the customer that any investment in the product or service is a good one.

Aspects of value

As the above examples illustrate, value can take a number of forms, depending on the specific customer circumstances. To create customer value for specific customers, each potential benefit needs to be identified and translated into value using words that the customer understands, ideally by translating the benefit into monetary value.

Good salespeople are very skilled at guiding the customer to work out the value of any potential benefit for themselves by prompting them to consider the areas of their business that would benefit. It is much more powerful for the customer to go through their own mental process to calculate the value that would accrue to them, rather than just being given a figure by someone else. Going through the calculation of value themselves creates a lasting impression in the mind of the customer.

As customers understand their business very well, an alternative strategy would be to advise the customer of the typical value of the benefit in question, making reference to similar organizations that have already used the product or service in question, and then ask the customer to estimate whether they are likely to experience similar value creation. Figure 4.4 illustrates all areas where value is created.

Value of cost reduction

The reduction of costs is a relatively easy benefit to translate into value as it is already stated in monetary terms. All those areas where cost savings can

FIGURE 4.4   Aspects of value

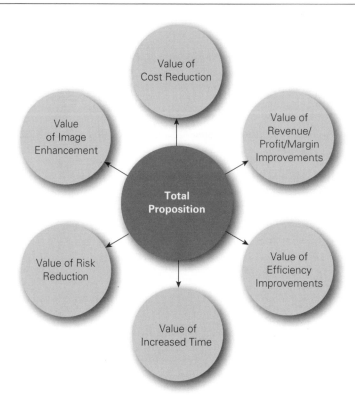

be had should be outlined to the customer, with the customer being asked to estimate the specific savings they might enjoy. Again, if customers cannot come up with estimates, examples of cost savings enjoyed by typical customers should be offered to prompt the customer for their own estimates. It is useful to further explore these cost benefits by breaking them down into specific time periods, by asking how much could be saved in a month, in one year or during the course of the product or service usage.

Value of revenue/profit/margin improvements

As with cost benefits, the value of benefits to revenue, profit and margin are relatively easy to communicate as they are already stated in monetary terms. All those areas where revenue or profit can be achieved should be outlined to the customer, with the customer being asked to estimate the specific amount they might enjoy. Again, if customers cannot come up with their own figures, examples from other customers should be offered as a prompt. These monetary benefits should then be explored further by asking how much extra could accrue in a month, in a year or over some other period.

Value of efficiency improvements

In any business, time is money, so any reduction in the time taken to carry out a task could have significant value. Therefore, any benefit to efficiency or productivity can be relatively easily translated into value through its effect on cost or revenue. A new machine, for example, can reduce production costs, increase output and require less maintenance, all of which have monetary value.

Transaction efficiency relates to how much quicker it is to carry out a specific task. These efficiencies can also be relatively easily translated into value in terms of cost, time and revenue.

Value of increased time

A further aspect of value is the freeing up of time. The time saved by a new product or service can be used to do something more valuable. This is particularly important with small businesses, where the owners may be able to use any additional time to create more overall value for the business. For example, providing a bookkeeping service for a small business might free up the owner to:

- spend more time with important customers;
- develop some new products or services;
- spend more time training key staff;
- play more golf.

Taking the example of spending more time with important customers, this could help secure their business or even create new business opportunities. With the bookkeeping example in mind, customers should therefore be helped to understand the value of having time to do something else by asking the following questions:

1 How much time do you spend on bookkeeping?
2 What else could you do with this time?
3 What would one piece of new business be worth?

In this way, the customer has been guided through the process of estimating how much time a bookkeeping service might save and the value that this service might bring.

Value of risk reduction

The ability of a proposition to reduce risk or to eliminate it entirely is very valuable. Some risks are of course considerable, such as the risk to life or the risk of losing the business.

The most effective approach to communicate the value of risk reduction is again to ask the customer to estimate the size of their own risk. To use the bookkeeping example again, an effective sales approach would be to ask the customer to estimate the risk of submitting incorrect figures to Her Majesty's Revenue & Customs.

Value of image enhancement

To enhance an individual's image and status is valuable and can often explain the purchase of expensive consumer goods. Image and status are also valuable to an organization, as they can enhance its appeal or reputation in the eyes of its customers.

This can be seen in the standard of buildings and furnishings used by those organizations that trade on their image and status. Again, the customer should be encouraged to estimate the value of an increased reputation in the marketplace in winning new business opportunities.

Value mapping

The total proposition can therefore produce a large number of features and potential benefits and create customer value in many different areas. Just as identifying the total proposition was a useful exercise in identifying all aspects of the organization's product and service offering, a *value mapping* exercise will be useful in identifying all possible benefits of each element or feature of this proposition, together with the customer value these can create.

Ideally, we should start with our key differentiators and then map the potential benefits and value they can create, as these aspects of the total proposition are unique to an organization and of considerable potential value to customers. Value mapping lists all elements of the total proposition – which are in fact features of the proposition – and looks to identify as many ways as possible in which they can each create benefits and customer value. Figure 4.5 reflects this process.

For example, Feature 1 of the proposition can create three separate customer benefits (Benefits 1, 2 and 3). Benefit 1 can then create three different aspects of value (Values 1, 2 and 3).

FIGURE 4.5   Value Mapping

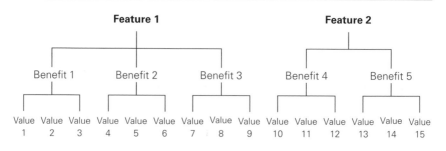

FIGURE 4.6   How an organization's proposition creates value for its customers

Feature 1			Feature 2	
Benefit 1	Benefit 2	Benefit 3	Benefit 4	Benefit 5
Value 1	Value 4	Value 7	Value 10	Value 13
Value 2	Value 5	Value 8	Value 11	Value 14
Value 3	Value 6	Value 9	Value 12	Value 15

The completion of the value mapping exercise will create a schedule that looks like the one in Figure 4.6. This represents one of the organization's most important assets – a complete analysis of how the organization's proposition can create value in the eyes of its customers.

Creating value propositions

The work done so far in identifying how a proposition can generate customer benefit and customer value will effectively become a toolbox from which to select the best tool when engaging customers. A *value proposition* identifies the net value of a specific customer proposal. It is effectively the difference between the customer's investment and the customer's return on this investment. It is the customer's net gain in acquiring and using the product or service in question.

It is possible to create any number of different value propositions from any combination of elements from the total proposition as part of the relationship the organization aims to develop with specific customers. This will of course depend on the specific requirements and expectations of each individual customer, and also on the type of relationship the organization wants to develop with different categories of customer. These are all issues we will explore in the next chapter, on the *sales process*.

The Value Balance Sheet

In any commercial exchange, the customer makes a calculation of value. This calculation can be intuitive, based on gut-feel, or it can be made as part of a more formalized process that brings together the total investment required and the extent of the expected return.

In both situations the customer normally has a fairly clear view of the cost of making a purchase, but more often than not has a less clear view of the possible returns on this investment. This lack of clarity may well explain the nervousness that customers often demonstrate during the purchase decision.

It is therefore the responsibility of the seller to make the best possible case to justify any purchase. The Value Balance Sheet diagram in Figure 4.7 illustrates this point.

FIGURE 4.7   Value Balance Sheet

Value created for customer	Customer investment
Value (V1)	Initial Cost
Value (V2)	Operating Cost
Value (V3)	Service Cost
Total Value	Total Investment

This figure represents the situation in the customer's mind when they consider both sides of the purchase equation. On the right-hand side of the Value Balance Sheet are all the elements of cost associated with the purchase. These include *initial purchase cost* and any other costs relating to the product's usage such as *operating costs* or *servicing costs*. These costs are usually well known to the customer.

The left-hand side of the Value Balance Sheet represents the total value created by all elements of the product and service under consideration. These elements may be less well appreciated by the customer.

It is therefore the responsibility of the seller to build up the left-hand side of the sheet as much as possible by creating the maximum amount of value in the mind of the customer. This is a high-level sales skill and requires a complete understanding of the customer's particular situation and their specific requirements and expectations. It also requires a complete understanding of all elements of the selling organization's total product and service offering and how all its various elements can create value for the customer.

The value proposition creator

Ideally, each customer will require a specific value proposition tailor-made to meet their particular requirements, and this is of course the essence of good sales strategy. The *value proposition creator* in Figure 4.8 can be used to develop any number of different value propositions.

FIGURE 4.8   The value proposition creator

Who is the target customer?	
What issues & aspirations do these customers have?	
What will your product or service do for them?	
Why should they prefer your offer over the competition?	
The elevator pitch	

Who is the target customer?

In the work done on customer strategy (see Chapter 3), specific customer groups were identified that the organization wanted to develop relationships with. It may therefore be decided that different value propositions should be created for different categories of customer. It may further be decided that these different categories of customer should be engaged with in different ways, and this will be reflected in the *sales process* in the next chapter. The *customer profiles* developed in the previous chapter will provide all the information needed for this exercise.

What issues and aspirations do these customers have?

The customer profiles should again provide most of the information needed to answer this question, which is posed to test the organization's level of understanding about this particular category of customer. In any event, the organization's knowledge of this category of customer should reflect the following:

- competitive activity in their marketplace;
- impact of economic, political, social and technological factors;
- typical customer concerns and issues.

What will your product or service do for them?

This question again emphasizes that customers are not interested in what the product or service is, but in what it can do for them. The work done in this chapter on the total proposition and the creation of customer value will allow the organization to answer this question very well for each category of customer.

Why should they prefer your offer over the competition?

This question probes the whole question of competitive advantage and what (if anything) the organization has that sets it apart or differentiates it from competitors. Again, the work done in this chapter on the total proposition, and in particular those aspects of the proposition referred to as *key differentiators* – those aspects that create the most customer value and where there is a competitive advantage – will provide everything needed to answer this question.

The elevator pitch

An *elevator pitch* is a short and punchy summary of the value proposition that could be given in a few seconds to someone in an elevator – hence the name. It is obviously an Americanism, but it does sound better than a *lift pitch*. An elevator pitch contains the essence of the value proposition and is in effect a shorthand version of all the work done so far on customer strategy and total proposition.

The ability to deliver an elevator pitch tests how tight and well thought through the value proposition is. If someone has difficulty in coming up with an elevator pitch, it is a good sign that not enough thinking has gone into its development.

Workshops and case studies

Some workshops and case studies can be found below that are designed to help the reader apply some of the techniques discussed in this chapter and to illustrate how organizations have coped with some of the issues involved.

WORKSHOP   The Value Proposition Workshop 1:
                Creating value propositions

Objective

This workshop is designed to stimulate the use of all the key techniques explored in this chapter, specifically *Total Proposition*, *Differentiator Matrix* and *Customer Value*, by asking those attending the workshop to create customer value propositions and to deliver an elevator pitch. This workshop also uses the *Customer Profiles* developed in Chapter 3 on customer strategy.

Process

1 Ask those attending the workshop to bring the customer profiles with them that identify the characteristics of the typical customers.

2 Split the team into smaller groups and ask each group to use the *value proposition creator* discussed earlier to create a value proposition for a specific category of customer.

3 Ask members of each group to deliver an *elevator pitch* in order to communicate the value proposition they created.

4 Keep repeating the exercise until you have created value propositions for all customer groups and have given each salesperson a number of opportunities to deliver an elevator pitch.

Key questions

- Do the value propositions create real value?

- Do they differentiate the organization from competitors?

- Do the salespeople sound convincing?

- Has the level of confidence within the team increased?

CASE STUDY   Value Proposition Case Study 1:
Commercial insurance provider – Identification of
total proposition and key differentiators

Background

The company provides commercial insurance to large organizations in the UK that covers them against most business risks. The organization markets its policies through a network of insurance brokers who manage the end customer relationship on its behalf. The company wanted to identify elements of its insurance offering that would provide competitive differentiation.

Activity

A series of workshops were conducted for all regional managers and their sales teams to utilize the total proposition methodology and the Differentiator Matrix to identify any competitive advantages. Once the key differentiators were identified, the account managers practised using them to create customer value in a series of role-play sessions utilizing the Value Balance Sheet.

Key learning points

- Prior to the workshop, most managers and account managers did not appreciate the full extent of their total product and service offering.

- The organization had a number of key differentiators but did not appreciate their full customer value and their competitive advantages.

- The Value Balance Sheet became a very strong concept in the mind of salespeople to ensure they remembered to create the maximum customer value in any commercial negotiation.

- The role-play sessions significantly increased the account managers' confidence in using their proposition to create customer value.

The sales process
How should we engage with our target customers?

05

FIGURE 5.1 The Business Performance Value Chain: Sales process

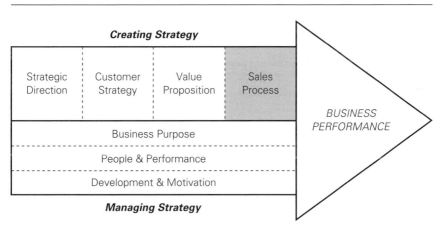

Sales process is the final part of the Business Performance Value Chain that relates to *creating strategy*. It brings to a focus all the work we have already done in Part Two to create a sales and customer strategy for the organization. This sales process will therefore be in line with the strategic direction of the organization in order to deliver the organization's value propositions to those customers that have been identified as important.

This sales process must ensure that the organization is doing the right things at the right times, particularly at those crucial points in the customer buying process when the sales interventions can be vital. The sales strategy should reflect the customer's buying process to enable the organization to influence and manage its progress from start to finish.

In this final chapter of Part Two we will therefore look at how the organization will engage with its different categories of customer, particularly with its smaller customers as part of *activity management*. We will also consider how this contrasts with the way it will engage with its larger customers as part of *account management*.

The sales process

In Chapter 3 on customer strategy we began by identifying a generic customer journey that included a number of key stages that all customers seem to move through as part of their buying process. These key steps were:

NEED – SEARCH – EVALUATION – DECISION – REVIEW

We then went on to identify the specific customer journey for target customers by identifying what actually happens at each stage of their buying process – what is important to them at each stage and who is involved. We therefore identified a decision-making process (DMP) and a decision-making unit (DMU) for these target customers.

To begin this section, we are going to take a similar approach by first identifying a generic sales process that reflects the typical customer buying process. We will then move on to identify the organization's own sales process in order to reflect and respond to the specific needs of its customers.

This sales process must be able to deliver the *value propositions* to the target customers in the most effective way. Given that different categories of customer may have been identified, requiring different types of relationship, we may therefore arrive at a situation where there are different sales processes selling different value propositions to different customers. This would be a very positive outcome as it would demonstrate that the full value is being extracted from the products and services, and that the business opportunities provided by all of the various categories of customer are being exploited.

The sales process diagram in Figure 5.2 reproduces the generic customer journey introduced in Chapter 3 and introduces those elements of sales process required in response. This sales process outlines the necessary actions needed to meet customer requirements and expectations at every stage of their buying process.

From Figure 5.2, we can see that there are certain stages that our sales strategy needs to follow in order to reflect the customer journey. These are:

FINDING – ENGAGING – PROVING – WINNING – KEEPING

FIGURE 5.2   Sales process

	Need	Search	Evaluation	Decision	Review
Customer Journey	*Having a Requirement*	*Looking for Help*	*Examining the Options*	*Making a Commitment*	*Evaluating Experience*
	Finding	*Engaging*	*Proving*	*Winning*	*Keeping*
Sales Process	*Searching*	*Opening*	*Features / Benefits*	*Objection Handling*	*Customer Satisfaction*
	Prospecting	*Analysis / Fact Find*	*Value Proposition*	*Trading Value*	*Relationship Development*
	Qualifying	*Summary & Vision*	*References*	*Negotiation*	*Added Value*

This is the entire sales process from beginning to end. It represents all the stages in a sale for new customers, from initial prospecting through to winning and keeping the business.

We will later adapt this sales process to respond to specific categories of customer as identified in the customer strategy and to reflect the situation where there might be a large number of small customers or a small number of large customers. In the former case, *activity management* is suggested, whereas *account management* is implied for the latter case.

Even for existing customers, new areas of their business may still need to be explored in order to sell additional products and services, or even to ensure that enough interest is being shown in them to warrant keeping their existing business over the longer term. Our sales strategy must therefore:

- *FIND* those customers who have a *NEED*;
- *ENGAGE* with customers who are *SEARCHING*;
- *PROVE* the value of our proposition when customers are *EVALUATING*;
- *WIN* the business when customers are making a *DECISION*;
- *KEEP* the business during any customer *REVIEW*.

Stages in the sales process

A sales strategy needs to be developed to ensure that all of the bases of the customer journey are covered. The organization must target the necessary sales resources at its chosen customers and ensure it manages those crucial customer moments of truth – those all-important tipping points that occur at various stages of their buying process.

Some customers will require considerable sales input, while others will require very little. Different categories of customers may also buy in very different ways, with different purchase criteria and buying processes. As we have already noted, this may lead to a different sales process for each category of customer, which will have important implications for sales structure, sales skills and sales management.

It is probably best to start with the most important customer category and develop a sales process for them. The organization may later find that it can get away with minor tweaking of this process for different categories of customer.

Finding

In this first part of the sales process the organization is trying to *FIND* those customers who have a *NEED*.

Searching and prospecting

All organizations need a steady stream of *customer leads* to feed into their sales process. The organization therefore needs a continuous process that scans the marketplace for potential customers in this early stage of their customer journey.

A major element of an organization's sales and marketing effort must be designed to create enough prospects (prospective customers) that will ultimately lead to actual customers, and to feed these prospects into the sales process. This number of prospects will depend upon the size of the ultimate sales objective, the average sales value of typical customers, and the typical conversion rates experienced as prospects move through the sales process. We will explore this in more detail when we look at *activity management* and *account planning* later in the chapter.

A traditional role for marketing has been to use advertising and promotion to attract potential customers in order to create leads for the sales organization. This role is still very important but the growth of the internet and other digital media has radically changed the marketing landscape.

Given that most customers can find hundreds of potential suppliers in 10 minutes on Google, the role of marketing has changed from *pushing* itself outwards towards the customer to *pulling* the customer towards the organization using a variety of means including online resources. This is particularly relevant in B2C where business can also be transacted online, but in the B2B space, where the transaction is more complex, the personal interaction provided by a salesperson or account manager is still required.

There has always been a role for salespeople to prospect their sales territories in order to find sales leads. As we will see when we take a close look at sales skills in Part Three, this remains a key element aspect of selling; however, organizations must also use other marketing techniques, including advertising, promotions, the internet and telemarketing, to assist with lead generation.

When we looked at customer strategy, we concluded the chapter by creating a number of customer profiles for each of the specific categories of customer. The purpose of these profiles was to provide a clear picture of these customers in order to focus the sales effort.

These profiles can also be used to guide prospecting, as the organization wants to find other potential customers that are similar in profile to the ones it is already dealing with. If the organization knows what it is looking for, the search process should be much easier.

An interesting question is whether or not potential customers can be pushed into the *need* phase. As discussed earlier, a need arises as a result of either a negative situation that the person or company wants to avoid, or a positive outcome that is sought. By introducing a new product or service that creates significantly more value than anything the customer currently has, a salesperson can create dissatisfaction with the current situation and a desire for something new. An effective sales process can thus create the motivation to change and therefore can be said to have created a need.

Qualifying

Customer leads come in all shapes and sizes – they come from many different types of customer with a variety of different business opportunities. We therefore need some criteria to separate the wheat from the chaff – we need qualification criteria.

Organizational fit

In Chapter 2 on strategic direction, the *distinctive competencies*, *market definition* and *competitive positioning* of an organization were developed. These defined what the organization is good at and where it wants to compete. In Chapter 3 on customer strategy, the *Customer Relationship Matrix* and *Customer Importance Mapping* were also utilized to identify that some customers and some types of business are more important than others, and *Customer Profiles* were developed to identify what these customers look like. The more a potential customer resembles one of these profiles, the more likely the organization is to win the business. These things should be borne in mind when qualifying leads to determine whether the potential business fits with what the organization is all about and where it wants to go.

Resources required to win the business

Sales resources, like any other scarce resources, need to be applied to those opportunities that provide maximum return. In addition to sales resources, other areas of the organization are often required to respond to customer enquiries and customer opportunities, which can put a huge strain on those areas that are already stretched by their normal activities.

Because some customer opportunities will be relatively easy to resource while others will not, organizations need to decide which opportunities to chase and which to leave alone, purely on the basis of the amount of time and money needed to convert them into business. As a result, it is quite normal for organizations to decline opportunities to bid for business purely on the basis of the extent of the response required.

Resources required to service the customer

A similar argument applies to the resources required to service this business once it is won, with some types of business being much harder to service than others. This can also be a factor in whether or not an opportunity survives this qualification process.

Business value and profitability

The overall value of the opportunity and its profitability are important factors in qualifying an opportunity. The type of business on offer is also an important factor. The organization may be looking to emphasize new product category areas or move into new areas of the market, and therefore opportunities to win business in these new areas would represent higher-value opportunities. However, high levels of potential business are certain to attract other competitors and will therefore reduce the overall chances of success.

Strategic business or customers

The winning of certain categories of business or the winning of particular customers may be important to enhance the status, credentials or reputation of the organization. This may help in developing business from other customers, who might be impressed with the type of business the organization conducts or with the stature of customer the organization usually deals with.

Business risk

Some types of business are more risky than others. This risk ranges from the customer who is always late paying their invoices, through to those customers where the amount of business is so large that any default in payment could threaten the survival of the organization. As a result of this type of risk, organizations often have tight rules relating to the provision of credit and to the size of their exposure to individual customers. These rules will be reflected in their qualification criteria.

Timescale

The timing of when the business could be placed is also an important factor. Those opportunities that are likely to happen soonest are of more interest than those that might arrive later. Opportunities that have a longer gestation period are often more problematic and less likely to come to fruition, as a lot can happen within the buying organization itself or to the external environment that may impact on any requirement.

Competitive activity

The probability of winning a specific piece of business is related to a number of factors. The strength of competition in a particular marketplace or for a particular customer will have a strong impact upon the chances of success. Quite simply, the more competitors that are involved, the less likely an organization is to be successful.

Furthermore, the relative financial health of competitors can also force them into certain actions that are more related to the state of their cash flow than to anything else. This could lead to competitors offering deals and terms that cannot be matched. Coming up against competitors in this situation is therefore an issue that should be evaluated in the qualification process.

The strength of any previous relationship the organization has had with the potential customer is another factor. These customer experiences with the organization, or any individual within it, can of course be positive or negative.

The strength of any relationship between the potential customer and a competitor is also important. A competitor with an existing relationship with the customer is normally in a much stronger position and any enquiry that another organization receives may only represent the customer testing out the market from time to time.

The match between the potential customer's need and an organization's value proposition is another important factor. If the organization can demonstrate that its proposition can create more value for the customer than any competitive offering, then it is in a strong position. However, if its proposition creates less value than a competitive offering, then it is of course in a much weaker position. This point just emphasizes the importance of understanding the customer requirement and tailoring the product and service to create the most value for the customer – aspects already explored in Chapters 3 and 4 on customer strategy and the value proposition.

Another important factor impacting upon success is the stage in the buying process that the potential customer is at when the organization first makes contact. The earlier the organization makes contact in the customer's buying process, the greater its chance of success.

At this early stage, the selling organization has the first opportunity to develop good relationships with key individuals in the customer organization who are involved in the buying process. This early involvement in the customer buying process also provides an opportunity to influence the very nature of the customer requirement, and to create a situation where the best solution to the customers' requirement is the organization's own proposition.

This represents the best possible case and will put the organization in *Position A* for getting the business. However, the worst case is where an organization arrives very late in a potential customer's buying process and one of its competitors is already in Position A.

There are normally some classic signs when this is the case, which include receiving a customer enquiry that needs to be answered yesterday or where you are only asked for prices. This can indicate that a customer is just testing whether they have got the best possible deal from their chosen supplier. These are normally good indications that you have received a very late invitation to the party that is little more than an afterthought.

The only strategy that will normally work in this situation is to try and change the game by creating sufficient doubt in the customer's mind that they stop the buying process and start from the beginning all over again. A good analogy is in bowls, where the last bowl from a competitor in a losing position is a *wrecking ball* that aims to knock all the better-positioned balls out of the way.

Overall chance of success

All of the above factors need to be taken into account during qualification. Therefore, organizations need to develop an appropriate formula that can be applied to all customer opportunities in order to evaluate their value and importance and rate their overall attractiveness. Most *customer relationship management (CRM)* systems have the capability to calculate this value from a range of different factors important to the organization. Hopefully, such efforts in *FINDING* potential customers should result in an appropriate number of qualified customer leads moving onto the next stage of the sales process.

Engaging

At this stage in the sales process, a number of potential customers have passed the qualification process. Therefore, in this second stage in the sales process organizations are trying to *ENGAGE* with customers who are *SEARCHING*.

Opening

This stage may be the first time that the seller has met the buyer, although it is possible that meetings took place during prospecting and qualifying. However, if we assume that this is the first meeting with the prospective customer, then this step is probably the most important in the sales process and can often set the tone for the entire relationship.

Analysis and fact-find

The key objective at this stage in the sales process is to find out as much as possible about the customer, particularly their business situation and their requirements and expectations of any product or service they might ultimately buy. It is also important to identify their expectations about the nature of any relationship they would expect to have with any potential supplier.

Quite a lot of information about the customer can be found in the various published sources that are available, but in the final analysis, there is no substitute for being in front of the customer and asking them the right questions to reveal their business situation and issues. Therefore, the skills of *questioning*, *listening* and *probing* are among the most important of all sales skills and are a prerequisite for high levels of sales performance. These are thus important aspects of the sales role and will be examined in detail in Chapter 7 on people and performance.

There is a tendency for all salespeople to skimp on this important stage in the sales process, as they are usually champing at the bit to talk about their own proposition. However, the best sales performers resist the urge to talk about themselves and their own organization until they have thoroughly explored the customer's situation.

From the customer's point of view, this is a key stage in their buying process. They want to be sure that the salesperson has clearly understood their particular requirements and can suggest an ideal solution to meet them, to avoid being sold an inappropriate product or service. This concern in the early part of the customer's buying process is all part of the customer's *purchase anxiety*, which exists at every stage in this buying process. The onus therefore rests upon the salesperson to lessen this anxiety at each stage of the sales process, but particularly in the early stages.

This stage is thus not just about identifying the customer's situation and their requirements and expectations, but also about creating credibility and trust with the buying organization that will set the tone for the entire sales process. By asking the right questions, listening to the answers and probing particular areas of interest, the salesperson shows a genuine interest in the customer's situation and also demonstrates a detailed knowledge of the kind of business issues facing the customer. In this way, the fact-find provides an opportunity to both understand the customer and to create an ongoing professional relationship.

A good analogy for this stage in the sales process is the initial doctor–patient discussion in medicine. When a patient enters the doctor's surgery, he or she expects their symptoms to be fully explored before any treatment is offered. Furthermore, the kind of questions asked by the doctor demonstrates their detailed knowledge and experience. Most patients would feel short-changed and suspicious of any potential remedy if these professional courtesies were not demonstrated.

Summary and vision of the future

When the salesperson is satisfied that they have fully explored the customer's situation, it is time to bring this stage of the sales process to a conclusion. The most effective way of doing this is to summarize the key points of the discussion, paying particular attention to the customer's requirements and expectations. This technique demonstrates that the salesperson has fully understood the customer's situation, but also prompts the customer to add anything important that they may have forgotten to mention.

The final element in this stage of the sales process is to provide the customer with a *vision of the future*. This is achieved by thanking the customer for disclosing their information and assuring them that it will lead to the development of an ideal solution that will perfectly meet their requirements. This vision of the future creates a powerful expectation in the customer for the next stage in the sales process, which includes the presentation of the recommended solution that will deliver this vision.

Proving

In the third part of the sales process, the organization is trying to PROVE the value of its proposition when customers are EVALUATING.

We have until this point of the sales process been talking about developing new customers. However, as we have previously discussed in Chapter 3 on customer strategy, existing customers probably provide the best opportunities for additional business. Any such opportunities can therefore be merged into the sales process at this point to join those opportunities from new customers.

Features/Benefits/Value proposition

We have previously looked in great detail at these elements in Chapter 4 on the value proposition and so are not going to repeat it all again here, except to reiterate the key point from that chapter: that customers are more interested in what your proposition does for them than in what your proposition consists of. They are therefore more interested in the value of your proposition to their organization than in a list of features you might provide.

References

References from other customers who have already successfully used your products and services are worth their weight in gold and are much more powerful than any amount of advertising or PR. Customers are more interested in what you have already done than in what you say you can do.

At this stage in the sales process, the provision of customer references or invites to other customer sites to see your product or service in action could just tip the balance of the sale. Every organization should therefore aim to build up a source of references and case studies that can be used by the sales team. This information should be part of an overall repository of sales collateral that includes details of the organization's total proposition, the customer profiles of its target customers, and the value map that specifies how each element of the total proposition can create customer value.

Winning

In this part of the sales process we are trying to WIN the business when customers are making a DECISION.

It is no good having the most perfect build-up play in football if you can't score goals. It is also fruitless to hit perfect approach shots in golf if you can't putt. Similarly, all of the good work in strategic direction, customer strategy and value proposition will come to nothing if an organization cannot win any business.

By this stage in the sales process, the organization has gone through the equivalent of a sales due diligence. The customer's requirements have been understood and an appropriate proposition presented in response. The organization has earned the right to win the business and should therefore expect to be successful. At this stage in the sales process, salespeople should not be shy about asking for the business and should expect to get it.

Objection handling

Objections strike fear into many salespeople:

- The majority of salespeople think it means the buyer is not going to buy.
- Quite a number think that by ignoring objections, they will go away.
- Some think that the best way to overcome objections is just to talk louder.

All of the above responses fail to appreciate the true nature of what a customer objection represents. A customer objection is at the very least a customer response and represents something that can be dealt with. The most difficult customers are those that provide no feedback during discussions and then provide no response when a salesperson asks for the order.

An objection can be many things. It can be a query about a specific aspect of the proposition; it can be a request for more information to justify the purchase to a superior; it can represent some doubt about a claim made about the product; and it can also represent a misunderstanding. Whatever the reason, the best way to deal with an objection is to get all the reasons for it out on the table and then to put the best possible case in response.

Negotiation/Trading value

Even when the buyer likes your product or service and wants to buy it, there is often still a round of negotiations to come before the contract is signed. This is often right at the end of the sales process and is often about price.

In Chapter 4 on the value proposition, we introduced the notion of the Value Balance Sheet with the aim of demonstrating that the seller must create as much value on their side of the balance sheet as they can. This creates a position of strength and allows for these elements to be traded in any negotiation. Trying to negotiate without anything to trade is tantamount to begging.

There are some guiding principles about negotiation as follows:

- Know your ideal position, your acceptable position and your walk-away position.
- Know the key things you must get from any negotiation and the things that are 'nice-to-have's.
- Know the limits of what you can trade and what you can't.
- Know the limits of what the buyer can trade and what they can't.
- If you envisage a long-term relationship with the buyer, make sure the negotiation ends with a win-win for both parties.

Keeping

In the final part of the sales process we are trying to *KEEP* the business during any customer *REVIEW*.

Customer satisfaction/relationship development/added value

All customers are under competitive attack and therefore the only way to protect a position with an existing customer is to keep developing that position with that customer. If an organization stands still, some other organization will move in and take the business.

Current suppliers are particularly vulnerable during times of review, where the customer periodically evaluates their satisfaction with a supplier. Other danger signals are when something major happens within the customer organization, such as when a crisis hits or when a key individual arrives or moves on.

Current suppliers must therefore remain vigilant and should always be looking to add even more value to the relationship. This might be in terms of introducing new solutions to old problems or strengthening the relationships at every level of contact between the two organizations.

Developing the sales process

The previous discussion identified the typical stages in a sales process and what is involved at each stage. The selling organization now needs to develop its own sales process for its particular customers to identify the various sales activities that need to be completed at each stage. In effect, the organization has to fill in the gaps in Figure 5.3 to ensure that it knows what to do at each stage.

An organization may end up with a number of different sales processes, depending on the nature of the customer relationships that it is looking

FIGURE 5.3   Sales process development

	Need	Search	Evaluation	Decision	Review
Customer Journey *Target Customers*	*Having a Requirement*	*Looking for Help*	*Examining the Options*	*Making a Commitment*	*Evaluating Experience*
Sales Process *What should we do?*	*Finding*	*Engaging*	*Proving*	*Winning*	*Keeping*

to develop with each category of customer. Having a specific sales process for each category of customer has a number of important implications for the sales and customer strategy. In particular, a sales process will help to:

- manage the sales pipeline more effectively;
- maximize sales opportunities;
- identify where sales effort should be applied;
- identify when management intervention is required;
- make more accurate sales forecasts.

To develop the necessary sales processes for particular customers, the work on customer strategy should be revisited as a reminder of the categories of customer identified and their relative importance. The Customer Relationship Matrix was first used to identify four different categories of customer:

- Category 1 customers required a *transactional relationship*;
- Category 2 customers required a *negotiated relationship*;
- Category 3 customers required a *consultative relationship*;
- Category 4 customers required a *collaborative relationship*.

Customer Importance Mapping was then used to evaluate the relative importance of all customers in each of the four categories to identify whether they should be key accounts or development accounts. Key accounts represent the most important customers, while development accounts have the potential to become key accounts.

Activity management and account management

Activity management is implied where there are a large number of relatively small customers and all of these customers are of approximately equal importance. *Account management*, on the other hand, is implied where there are a relatively small number of larger customers who are all important.

From this basic analysis, we normally find that activity management is appropriate for those customers requiring a transactional relationship and account management for key accounts and development accounts. These are not hard and fast rules and the decision requires judgement. It may also be the case that both types of sales process are required, with some customers requiring activity management and some customers requiring account management.

Activity management

If there are a large number of small customers, activity management can ensure customers are progressed through the sales process to maximize the chance that sales targets are hit. Figure 5.4 illustrates this sales process and includes all of its stages from *finding* to *keeping*. This type of sales process is also often described as the *sales funnel* or *sales pipeline*, as it identifies the progress of customers through each stage in the sales process and also quantifies the success rate from one stage to the next.

Activity management is effectively a numbers game. The organization is trying to fill the top of the funnel with as many leads as possible to ensure enough of them survive and result in sufficient business being won to allow

FIGURE 5.4   Activity management: Transactional/opportunistic/maintenance accounts

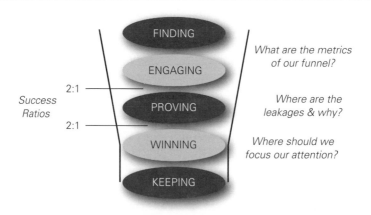

sales objectives to be met. The sales funnel therefore allows sales activity to be controlled in order to realize those advantages identified earlier:

- to manage the sales pipeline more effectively;
- to maximize sales opportunities;
- to identify where sales effort should be applied;
- to identify when management intervention is required;
- to make more accurate sales forecasts.

In order to utilize the sales funnel effectively, an organization needs to know the typical success rates at each stage in the funnel and the average order size. From this information, it can calculate how many prospects are needed to fill the funnel, how many can be expected to survive at each stage, and finally how many can be expected to produce orders. Managers can then intervene when necessary if the numbers fall short at any stage.

Example

If the success ratios in Figure 5.4 are used and it is assumed that the average order size is £2,000 and the sales target is £100,000, then the following activity must be ensured in order to hit target:

To hit target, 50 customers are needed with an average order value of £2,000, giving £100,000.

As the success ratio in the stage from *proving* to *winning* is 2:1 (half of them are lost at this stage), 100 customers are needed at the start of this stage, worth an estimated value of £200,000 (100 × £2,000).

As the success ratio from *engaging* to *proving* is also 2:1 (half of them are again lost at this stage), 200 customers are needed at the start of this stage, worth an estimated value of £400,000 (200 × £2,000).

Over the course of a year, the organization therefore needs to find 200 potential customers worth £400,000 to fill the sales funnel in order to end up with 50 customers and £100,000-worth of business.

Implications of activity management for salespeople

The type of sales activity required to engage effectively with customers and win their business under activity management calls for a specific type of salesperson. They must be willing to make a significant number of sales visits every day and must expect to be successful by winning orders in a significant number of them.

This type of sales activity will suit some individuals more than others, particularly those who respond to the instant gratification of taking orders on a regular basis. Such individuals might be less happy in a sales environment where customer business only materializes after a long and involved sales process, as characterized by larger customers with account planning.

Managers should recognize these differences when selecting individuals for these very different sales roles. In the case of activity management, they must ensure that they have a sufficient number of salespeople with the required sales skills to engage with enough customers to produce the required sales performance.

We will examine these issues further when we look at *sales structure* in Chapter 7 on people.

Implications of activity management for sales management

Management can use activity management as a diagnostic device to identify what is going on and to intervene as appropriate. If there are not enough leads going into the top of the sales funnel and not enough potential customers are being *engaged*, then attention should be directed at *searching*, *prospecting* and *qualifying*. This could also mean that marketing activity is not successful in providing enough sales leads.

If not enough potential customers are moving from *engaging* to *proving*, then not enough proposals are being presented. This could again suggest poor qualification or imply that salespeople are not identifying the specific requirements of customers or interesting them in their proposition.

If too few potential customers are moving from *proving* to *winning*, this could suggest that salespeople are not creating enough value in their customer propositions, failing to handle objections, or not fully trading the value of their proposition in any negotiation. Management would therefore need to investigate the possible causes of these issues, probably by observing salespeople in action.

Given the type of sales situation implied by activity management, managers can also use some of the more traditional methods of control for such activity, such as *call rate* and *strike rate*. Call rate is the number of customer contacts made in a specific time period and strike rate is the proportion of customer contacts that result in an order being taken.

Account management (Key account planning)

In this section, we are going to look at the most appropriate way of managing an organization's most important customers and target customers. We have previously identified these as either key accounts or development accounts in the work with the Customer Relationship Matrix and customer importance mapping.

These accounts are so important that they need to be given very individual attention and this means developing an *account plan* just for them. An account plan is both a planning document and a strategy document, as it is used to develop a plan of action for a particular customer. The role of an account plan is therefore to specify the sales process to be followed for a

FIGURE 5.5   Key account planning (KAM):
Key accounts and development accounts

specific customer. This joint role of planning and strategizing is represented by Figure 5.5, which identifies the key elements of such a plan.

A complete account plan would also contain information relating to the account in question, such as account history, sales history and key contacts (as indicated by *current situation* at the start of the process). However, we are going to concentrate on the planning and strategy aspects of key account planning in this section.

Overall goal

There must be an overall goal for each account – some ultimate objective. This goal should be appropriate and realistic and can range from establishing a presence with this customer, right through to winning the majority of this customer's business.

A *goal* in account planning is similar to a *vision* in strategic direction, as both provide an ultimate aiming point for strategy. In account planning, it provides the essential question for any activity by allowing you to ask: *Will this take the account nearer to my goal?*

Objectives and strategy

It is not usually possible to jump from the *current situation* to the *overall goal* in one leap. The movement towards an overall goal normally takes a series of separate steps over a period of time.

These steps are the same as those identified in the generic sales process discussed earlier: *engage*, *prove*, *win* and *keep* (*find* is excluded, as this account has already been identified as important). In key accounts and development accounts, the time needed to move from one stage to the next can be considerable. These stages can be represented as a series of individual objectives that move nearer to the overall goal.

If for example we are at the first stage (*engage*), the following objectives might be identified:

- Objective 1 – Identify possible contacts
- Objective 2 – Make initial contact
- Objective 3 – Identify customer issues and identify key contact

Each of these objectives will require a particular strategy to achieve them. The results of these strategies will then influence the choice of the next objective and strategy in the subsequent stages of *prove*, *win* and *keep*.

Time frame

Whereas the complete sales process for transactional accounts can be completed in a matter of seconds or minutes, in the case of key accounts or development accounts, this sales process can take months or even years to complete. Figure 5.5 illustrates this time element by breaking down the time interval from the current situation to the overall goal into four quarters. In reality this time interval could be much longer.

Resources

An account plan will need time in order to execute it properly. Some accounts will require the full-time attention of an account manager or even an account team.

The only way to identify how much time an account will need to exploit its full potential is to estimate the time requirement for each aspect of account strategy. Providing the potential of the account has been correctly identified (hence the need to evaluate customer importance in *customer strategy*), the return from this investment of time should be well worthwhile.

Other resources that the account plan may require for its implementation may include:

- specific expertise from somewhere within the organization or even outside of it;
- funding or budget;
- additional assistance from other areas of the organization;
- management support to help provide the necessary resources.

An account plan is a working document. It is meant to focus sales activity towards an overall goal and to measure progress towards its achievement.

Business buyer behaviour

The account plan represents the sales process for a particular customer and has to respond to the complexity of large customers and the uncertainties of

FIGURE 5.6   Business buyer behaviour: the decision making unit (DMU)

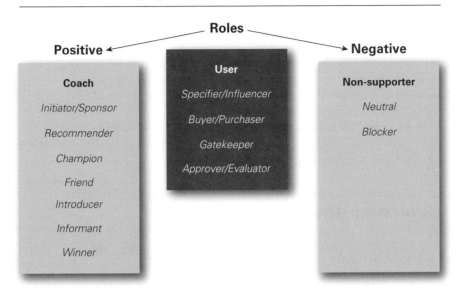

the commercial environment. It has to deal with the numerous individuals within the customer organization, often from different departments and often with conflicting roles, motivations and agendas. It also has to deal with the sudden changes of policy, strategy or priorities that can occur within these customers and even with the changing priorities and strategies of our own organization.

In this next section, we are going to examine one particular element of business buyer behaviour – the *decision making unit (DMU)*. The DMU represents all of the key players in an account and examines their roles and their impacts on the decision-making process. Figure 5.6 illustrates the constituents of a typical DMU.

DMU roles

- A *user* is an individual or group of individuals who will use the product or service in question.
- A *specifier* or *influencer* is an individual or group of individuals who create the criteria by which any purchase will be evaluated or who influence any aspect of the purchase decision.
- A *buyer* or *purchaser* is the individual who has the final say in any purchase decision.
- A *gatekeeper* is an individual who stands guard over the purchase process, either allowing or denying access to any aspect of the decision process.

- An *approver* or *evaluator* tests the product or service to ensure it meets requirements.

Individuals in the above roles can either be positively or negatively inclined towards the organization. A *coach* is a positive influence and supports the organization in any purchase decision by acting as *initiator, sponsor, recommender, champion, friend, introducer, informant* or *winner*. As will be seen in *development account entry strategy* below, the identification of such a supportive individual is crucial, whereas non-supportive influences can hinder or block progress in the account.

A key part of any account plan is therefore the identification of the above roles in a DMU and the development of a strategy to deal with them effectively.

Choice of development account

Even within the total number of development accounts that have been identified, there are some accounts that are even more approachable and responsive than others. These are the ones that should be approached first, as the chance of being successful is greater, which in turn can create a momentum of success and an appetite to win even more business.

A theory that was developed for the adoption of new technology products into the marketplace can have important implications for which development accounts are approached first. There are some customers that are more likely to be responsive to the proposition than others, particularly if the product or service in question is new and unique to the marketplace. These customers are typically less risk averse, more likely to try new approaches to old problems, more responsive to change and more likely to listen to new ideas.

Figure 5.7 identifies how certain types of customer respond to new ideas over time.

Innovators

This is probably the smallest group of customers, representing only 2.5% of all customers. However, *innovators* are the most eager to try anything new and will respond positively to new products and services and to new ways of doing business.

Early adopters

Early adopters are very similar to innovators and represent about 13.5% of all customers. They will also respond positively to new product ideas and new ways of doing business.

FIGURE 5.7   Customer responsiveness

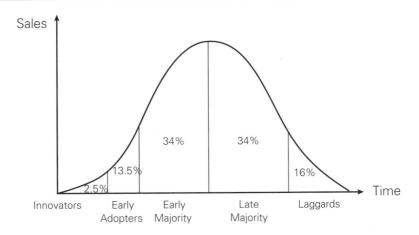

Early majority

The *early majority* are characterized by a more conservative nature and are less likely to try new products or new ideas. They typically wait until the innovators or early adopters have tried new things first and have sorted out any early issues. They are a much larger group of customers (34%) than the two earlier groups and are therefore responsible for much of the volume of business in any market.

Late majority

This group is probably as large as the early majority group (34%) and are even more conservative. The *late majority* will also wait until others have tried new products or ideas before they try them themselves. They are again responsible for a large proportion of the sales volume in any particular market, which makes them another important group.

Laggards

The *laggards* are the sceptics of the marketplace and are very unlikely ever to accept new ideas or new ways of doing business. They are probably the dinosaurs of any marketplace and will likely be the first group of customers to disappear.

For those organizations bringing new or unique products to the marketplace, it might therefore be advantageous to identify those customers that have a history of being the first to try new ideas and to target them initially. Success with these customers will then open up the rest of the market.

Development account entry strategy

The previous section should hopefully have helped to identify the development accounts to go for first. In this section, the entry strategy for these accounts will be identified.

Unlike key accounts, where there has been a prior relationship, development accounts are those where there may not have been much of a prior relationship, but there are significant opportunities for new business. As the organization has limited information about these customers, the first objective is to gain an understanding of what these customers are all about.

There is only one place that good information can come from and that is from inside the account itself. Therefore, someone within the account is needed to provide this vital intelligence as a prelude to developing account strategy designed to achieve the business objectives.

When we looked at the decision-making unit (DMU), we identified a particular role in the account that we called a *coach*. Such an individual usually has a personal reason or a business reason for helping a selling organization; that is, there is a specific advantage gained by them if the organization becomes a supplier.

A coach can only be found by networking around the customer organization until one is found, although they are often found early on in the investigation process. A coach can help by:

- Informing the selling organization about key issues and requirements of their business.
- Identifying who really makes the decisions.
- Helping to manoeuvre around certain obstacles.
- Identifying what stage the buying process has reached.
- Alerting the status of competitors.
- Arrange introductions to key individuals.
- Talking about the selling organization favourably.
- Informing how the organization and its offer is being perceived.
- Identifying potential blockers.

A coach with inside knowledge and information is therefore worth its weight in gold and should be cultivated whenever possible.

Implications of account planning for salespeople

Account planning calls for a specific type of salesperson who is able to take a more strategic or longer-term view of customer development. This type of sales activity will probably not suit those salespeople who crave the instant gratification of taking orders on a regular basis. Managers should therefore recognize these differences when selecting individuals for account planning roles. We will look more at these issues in *sales structure* in Chapter 7 on people.

Implications of account planning for sales management

In activity management, there are a relatively high number of customers passing through the sales process in a relatively short amount of time. In this situation, managers can measure sales activity and sales performance relatively easily by using the sales funnel to identify what is happening at each stage in the sales process and whether sales targets are being achieved.

This is not possible with account planning, where there are a small number of large accounts being managed and where these accounts may not produce sales results for some considerable time. In this situation, the most important sales management tool is the account plan itself, as it indicates both activity and progress. Without such a tool, managers would not be able to measure progress in these important accounts and would be reduced to just hoping that end results would eventually be achieved.

We will discuss how managers control key account activity in Chapter 7 on performance. How they develop the competence and effectiveness of their account managers will be tackled in Chapter 8 on development.

Time and territory management

The two biggest issues responsible for poor time and territory management among salespeople are first a lack of understanding about which customers are the most important and deserving of priority, and secondly the wasting of too much time on non-sales activity.

Customer priorities

A significant amount of sales resource is wasted by not providing customers with the appropriate levels of sales support and attention. Some customers receive too much, while others receive too little. What is required is a process that identifies customer importance and priorities, which then drives the salespeople's time allocation. The work done on customer importance and priorities in Chapter 3 on customer strategy will go a long way to ensuring that sales resources are focused on the areas of best opportunity.

Non-sales activity

If you ask most salespeople where they spend their time, you will find that a significant amount of time is spent on non-sales activity, particularly on administration, travelling and internal meetings. It is quite common for the majority of a salesperson's time to be spent on these activities, leaving precious little time for them to do what they should be doing, which is developing relationships with customers and selling the organization's products.

A very useful exercise is to ask salespeople to log the time they spend on all of their various activities and to identify where most of the non-sales time is going. Specific targets can then be agreed to increase selling time.

Automating the sales process

Recent advances in technology have created a number of products that can assist in the management of customers. Of most relevance to the sales issues discussed in this book are those products associated with *customer relationship management (CRM)* and *sales force automation*.

CRM is principally concerned with managing customer information and making it available to any individual in the organization to assist them in making an appropriate response to any customer issue. CRM systems can also record the details of transactions with customers and thus keep an up-to-date record of the customer relationship. Sales force automation is similar to CRM, as it provides the means to record all relevant customer information and customer transaction data in order to provide salespeople with accurate and up-to-date information.

Both of these systems can be programmed to highlight customers that fit a specific profile or to identify customers that might be interested in a new sales initiative. Both of these systems can also log any specific follow-up action that has been arranged for the customer at some future date.

Perhaps the most important lesson that organizations have learned from investing in such technology is to first design the sales process that the technology is supposed to enhance. A classic mistake is to invest in the technology and then try to fit the process around it, which often results in confusion, resistance and poor results.

Workshops and case studies

A number of workshops and case studies can be found below. These are designed to help the reader apply some of the techniques discussed in this chapter and to illustrate how organizations have coped with some of the issues involved.

WORKSHOP   Sales Process Workshop 1:
Developing the sales process

Objective

In this workshop the various sales processes will be defined that allow an organization to engage with its target customers in the most effective way to manage their buying process. The sales process for each target customer profiled in customer strategy will be developed.

It may be that each type of customer buys in a different way and therefore the sales process needs to reflect this. If these differences in buying behaviour are not significant, it is possible to develop a common sales process for all customers with minor variations for each type of customer.

Process

1 Ask those attending the workshop to go back to the flip chart that details the customer journey/buying process for a particular category of customer.

2 They should reproduce the sales process development box from page 87 on a new flip-chart sheet (landscape) and write the headings (*finding, engaging, proving, winning, keeping*) across the top.

3 Now ask them to fill in each of these boxes on the sheet as outlined below.

Key questions

FINDING

At this stage, the aim is to decide on the best way to identify customers at the time when their need occurs:

- Should a *come-to* strategy be operated that ensures information about products and services can be obtained easily from various sources such as the web? And/or

- Should a continuous *go-to* contact strategy be operated via e-mail, telephone or face-to-face means that keeps the organization in front of prospective customers?

ENGAGING

At this stage of the sales process, the aim is to decide how to best engage with customers in order to create a positive early impression, which will also facilitate all the later stages of the sale:

- What should the initial approach be? Invite to an exhibition or demonstration? Invite to a customer reference site? Arrange to meet someone within the prospect organization to conduct a fact-find?

- Should a *credentials presentation* be used that illustrates who we are/what we do/ what we have done?

- Should there be a standard template for a fact-find that allows identification of all the information needed at this stage of the sale?

PROVING

At this stage, the aim is to ensure that value propositions can be presented in a powerful and convincing fashion to target customers:

- Is there a schedule of all the various features of the total proposition and how these can create potential benefits and value for customers?
- Are the salespeople skilled in developing and presenting powerful customer value propositions?
- Is there a list of references or case studies that can be shared with prospects and customers that demonstrate the organization's capabilities?

WINNING

At this stage, the aim is to ensure that opportunities can be converted into business when customers are in decision mode:

- Are salespeople trained in the key sales skills of objection handling, trading value and negotiation?

KEEPING

At this stage, the aim is to ensure that the organization can keep and develop its customers to preserve and grow their business, particularly with key accounts:

- Is customer satisfaction with overall service levels and their relationship with the organization measured?
- Is there a process for monitoring changes in either personnel or strategies within key accounts?
- Are there other areas of need within customers that could be satisfied with additional products and services?

CASE STUDY   Sales Process Case Study 1:
UK provider of mailing services – Developing key account planning

Background

The company provides mailing services to most business customers in the UK and maintains a nationwide logistics network with sorting offices and delivery depots. The business is organized around a number of sales regions with its own sales and customer service organization focusing on serving customers in the specific geographical area covered by the region. The organization wanted to develop a key account organization that took a more national view of managing its key customers, rather than a purely regional view that managed all customers in the same way irrespective of their size and importance.

Activity

1 A review of customers was undertaken to identify those whose mailing requirements represented a very large part of the overall business and those where the customer's mail handling requirements did correspond to a national pattern of operations.

2 A number of key account managers were recruited from the existing sales organization on their suitability for managing the more complex customer buying process of larger customers.

3 A national key accounts organization was established outside of the control of the regional locations, which was responsible for growing the business of each account.

4 A key account planning process was established that created a common template for account planning for each account.

5 Management were trained to adopt a different management style for controlling the key account managers, which reflected the more complex sales process and the longer timescales for winning business.

6 Key account managers were trained in key account planning, particularly managing the *decision making process* (DMP) and the *decision making unit* (DMU).

Key learning points

- The selection process to identify key account managers was managed at an assessment centre and based around the identification of those competencies thought to be more relevant to managing large customers.

- The new strategy had to balance national account management of the customer relationship against the regionally based nature of customer delivery operations. This required the key account managers to spend as much time managing the internal relationship with regional locations as managing the external customer relationship.

- The key account planning document was changed from being a large document that mainly contained customer information into a working document that facilitated the development of account strategy, particularly the breaking down of the overall goal for the customer into a series of specific objectives.

- Sales resources were also needed in the regional locations to assist with the management of national customers, which led to the sharing of some of the national revenue gains with the regional locations.

CASE STUDY   Sales Process Case Study 2:
Truck manufacturer – Improving time and territory management

Background

The organization sells trucks through an independent dealer network across the UK and is tasked to maintain relationships with all of the major hauliers and owners of large truck fleets in the UK. The company wanted to ensure that its sales executives spent their time in the most efficient way in the pursuit of sales objectives.

Activity

1   Sales executives were asked to log all their activities over a two-week period and to break them down into the main categories of *customer planning, sales meetings, travelling, internal meetings, administration, holidays* and *sickness.*

2   A workshop was then arranged to discuss the findings from the analysis and to agree future action.

3   Following this meeting a minimum target was agreed that 55% of all available time should be spent on customer planning or sales meetings.

4   It was also agreed to develop a process for identifying customer importance and priorities that would be used across the entire sales organization.

Key learning points

- The main finding of the analysis was that only 40% of total time was actually spent on sales and customer development, with the remainder being spent on administration, travelling and attending internal meetings. This analysis came as a significant shock to both sales executives and sales managers.

- Another major finding of the analysis was that customer priorities based on customer importance and future business potential were not clearly understood across the sales team, which often meant that sales time was being spent in the wrong places. This led to the major project discussed above to develop a process for identifying customer importance and customer priorities.

CASE STUDY   Sales Process Case Study 3: Provider of automated search enquiries to solicitors and developers – Using the sales funnel for sales forecasting

Background

The company provides an online process for tracking property searches for solicitors and developers, which speeds up the whole process and keeps more accurate and updated records of the process of any search. The company wanted to develop a common sales process that could be used by the entire sales team. It needed to reflect the typical customer buying process and utilize best practice to engage with these customers in the most effective way.

Activity

1   As part of a facilitated workshop for the whole sales team, a common sales process was developed that matched a typical customer buying process.

2   This sales process had a series of specific stages that reflected the progress of a typical sale from initial contact through to the signing of contracts.

3   A series of estimated probabilities was attached to each stage of the sale to enable more accurate sales forecasts to be made.

Key learning points

- The sales team created their own sales process during the workshop based on their own experience of working with customers. This created complete ownership and acceptance of the sales process by those who would ultimately use it.

- As more information was gained from monitoring the sales process over a period of time, the estimated probabilities were changed to reflect actual experience, which made the sales forecasts even more accurate.

- Management also used the information coming from the sales process to identify why certain categories of sale were not progressing to a successful conclusion and developed a revised service for certain categories of customer in response.

PART THREE
Managing Strategy

In Part Two we started with strategic direction to provide the focus for all other aspects of creating strategy. Similarly, in Part Three we will start with *business purpose*, which will provide the essential underpinning for all other aspects of managing strategy and in particular the importance of leadership in creating the organization's culture.

In Chapter 7 on people and performance we will then consider how to create an organization that is fit for purpose and is kept pointing in the right direction. Finally, in Chapter 8 on development and motivation we will look at how managers extract the full potential of all those in the organization to create outstanding performance.

FIGURE 6.1 The Business Performance Value Chain: Managing strategy

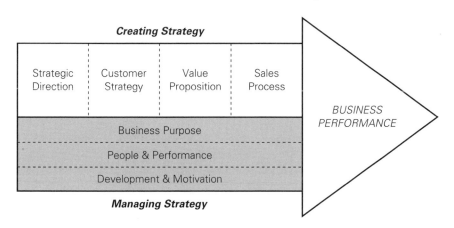

Business purpose
What kind of organization do we want to be?

06

A sense of *business purpose* forms the essential glue that holds an organization together. This business purpose provides the organization with the necessary inner strength and resolve to move towards its vision and overall goals, whilst withstanding the uncertainties of the external environment and attacks from competition. In essence, business purpose creates the overall framework in which the organization will deliver its sales and customer strategy and provides the necessary impetus to help it get there.

An organization's business purpose defines the organization and everything it believes in. As such, it can be defined as the essential reason why the organization exists. The term business purpose is synonymous with *business mission*, but due to the common confusion between vision and mission, the term business purpose is preferred in this book.

We previously discussed in Part Two the importance of strategic direction in setting out the organization's vision and overall goals. Strategic direction and business purpose therefore come together to provide the most important drivers of organizational behaviour, setting out both what the organization believes in and where it wants to go.

It is important that these key drivers of organizational direction reinforce each other rather than conflict. For example, if one aspect of an organization's core competences is related to excellent customer relations and after-sales service (part of strategic direction), then this should be reflected in the belief that internal staff should be treated with fairness and respect (part of business purpose). If this is not the case, customers are hardly likely to receive the service that the organization expects them to receive.

The author's consultancy work with clients in various industry sectors has confirmed the importance of both strategic direction and business purpose in providing the essential benchmarks by which to assess business performance and success. Senior managers responsible for strategy development within their organizations should therefore give these aspects particular attention and ensure that they have been properly communicated. This sense of purpose can take many forms, as outlined below.

A desire to survive

Peter Drucker, an influential business writer, once said that *the main business of any business is to stay in business*. The desire to survive is a fundamental part of any organization's business purpose and is reflected in many of the actions it takes. These actions are particularly obvious when painful decisions have to be made in response to changes in economic conditions or to movements in customer demand.

This survival instinct also has a positive connotation as it forces organizations to evolve over time in response to these same external influences. This leads to the view that in order to survive, organizations cannot stand still but must continually evolve and develop over time.

A desire to grow

Sometimes growth itself is the overriding business purpose, where size, particularly large size, is often seen as an objective in its own right. Perhaps this motivation is related to the previous element of survival, where bigger is seen to be safer, or to the fact that financial rewards within most organizations appear to increase in response to larger scale. Whatever the reasons, the desire to grow is certainly an important element in most organizations' business purposes.

A desire to innovate

Some organizations seem to have been created with the sole intention of pushing the boundaries in either new product development or in new ways of doing business. The likes of Apple and Amazon quickly come to mind as examples of organizations that have taken innovation to its fullest extent to change the way we operate digital devices and how we purchase goods and services. This philosophy of innovation and creativity is a clear element of their business purpose, which influences everything these organizations do.

A desire to wield power and influence

Some organizations seem to regard power and influence as key drivers of their behaviour. Whether it is to change the world for good or bad, they just want to be heard and listened to. Certainly some of the large media corporations appear to be following this model of organizational purpose and have amassed vast global empires to this end.

A desire to serve

The desire to be of service to a specific community or to society in general is another key element of some organizations' business purpose. Such a philosophy also extends to a desire to serve specific customers, and an entire organization may be structured around this one purpose. This book is predicated on the view that sales and customer strategy should drive all aspects of the organization, so this desire to serve customers and to provide them with an experience in line with their expectations can provide a very strong focus for an organization.

A desire to provide opportunities for others

Some organizations have clearly been set up to address specific social or political issues or to provide opportunities for the more vulnerable elements in society. Even those organizations with a more commercial focus often believe that a key element of their purpose is to provide opportunities for employment and personal growth. A philosophy where organizational objectives are aligned with the personal objectives of individuals is a key motivational tool and we will examine this in more detail in Chapter 8 on motivation.

A desire to make money

The desire for financial rewards is certainly a key aspect of why many commercial organizations were formed in the first place. Put simply, they were formed to make the original owners (and subsequent shareholders) some money.

Although this sounds like a selfish doctrine, it does embody the fundamental principle on which capitalism is based, namely that entrepreneurship is the key driver of commercial success and future prosperity. Indeed, capitalism as an economic philosophy believes that the utilization and allocation of all scarce resources is best served by the dynamics of market forces.

Furthermore, economic theory relating to how commercial organizations operate assumes they will always try to maximize returns on their investment. The so-called *theory of the firm* that all students learn in Economics 101 assumes that all firms will always attempt to maximize profits.

It is of course possible to have a mix of all the above elements that come together to define an organization's business purpose, but the above discussion raises an important question for all organizations: *What is your business purpose?*

Strategy and business purpose

We have already discussed the idea that strategic direction and business purpose should be mutually supportive. Figure 6.2 illustrates this point further by identifying the different value delivery strategies that organizations can adopt as part of their overall strategic direction. It is important to understand what these options imply for an organization trying to deliver these strategies.

FIGURE 6.2   Business strategy and business purpose

Aspects of Organization	Value delivery strategies		
	Operational excellence	Product leadership	Customer intimacy
Business Process	Sharp distribution systems providing no hassle service	Nurtures ideas into effectively marketed products	Provides solutions and helps customers run their business
Structure	Strong central authority with finite level of empowerment	Acts in an ad-hoc, loosely knit & ever-changing way	Pushes empowerment close to human contact
Management Systems	Standard operating procedure	Reward individuals innovation and new product success	Measures cost of customer service & maintaining loyalty
Culture	Acts predictably with one size fits all	Experiments & thinks out of the box	Flexible – have it your way
Examples	McDonalds	3M	Ritz Carlton Hotels

Operational excellence

Organizations focusing on operational excellence will have strong central authority and standard operating procedures. Such organizations are effectively process driven and allow very limited flexibility in any aspect of organizational activity or behaviour. Process, structure and management systems within these organizations will be centrally determined and utilized wherever the organization operates, irrespective of geography.

In these organizations the overriding culture will be one of standardization, with predictable responses to all conceivable situations. People within these organizations will be expected to follow rules and procedures and will be rewarded for doing so. They will not be expected to create changes to any aspect of internal process, and nor will they be expected to think outside the box in any way.

Product leadership

Organizations focusing on product leadership, on the other hand, will be totally different. They will place a high value on new ideas and original thinking to encourage the development of the new product ideas that are vital for their success. Process, structure and management systems within these organizations will be flexible and loose, perhaps even non-existent, as formal devices to control activity and behaviour are seen as obstacles to creativity and the flow of ideas.

Unlike those working in organizations focusing on operational excellence, employees in product-led organizations will be encouraged to innovate and to challenge traditional ways of thinking. This is a very different type of organizational culture from what would exist under operational excellence.

Customer intimacy

Finally, organizations focusing on customer intimacy or customer satisfaction will put a strong emphasis on providing customers with what they want and will seem to go out of their way to meet any reasonable customer requirement or expectation. Process, structure and management systems within these organizations will be somewhere between the two previous examples. They will be designed to push personal responsibility and decision making as far down the organization as possible to allow for the necessary flexibility of actions and behaviour.

These organizations typically operate in high-end service industries and require a totally different mindset from their employees. People in these organizations are given extensive authority and are empowered to act in any way that contributes to the satisfaction of their customers. They are not bound by rules and procedure and are expected to act with flexibility and autonomy.

It is clear from these examples that strategy and business purpose are inextricably linked, requiring a high degree of consistency between these two drivers of organizational strategy.

Culture

The organization's business purpose will be translated into action by all elements of sales and customer strategy. In this way, the essential purpose of the organization will be instrumental in forming the fabric of the business and defining its structure and core operating processes. There is, however, another key element that is required to facilitate this transfer of business purpose into organizational behaviour: *culture*.

The word culture crops up in a variety of different contexts, but as we are concerned about sales and customer strategy, culture can be defined as a pattern of shared assumptions about the organization and its environment. These assumptions can take many forms and they shape the way individuals and groups think and act within an organizational context.

Put simply, an organization's culture can be defined as *how we do things around here*. An organization's culture is therefore a collective term that describes what the organization believes in and what it values.

Beliefs and values

Beliefs can be defined as what the organization collectively perceives to be true, and *values* can be defined as what the organization collectively perceives to be important. These beliefs and values can relate to the organization itself or to anything related to the external environment.

Beliefs about the organization can include:

- what it considers it is good at doing and what it is not;
- what it believes its optimum size should be in terms of turnover and number of employees;
- where it believes it should operate in terms of geographical locations.

Beliefs about the external environment can include:

- a belief about the political, economic and social environment the organization faces now and in the future;
- a belief about the future needs and requirements of customers;
- a belief about the impact of technology development;
- a belief about the future nature and extent of competition.

As far as values are concerned, these can relate to employee rights and participation, charitable giving, or any aspect of race, health, gender or sexual orientation. The organization can also have values relating to customer service, business ethics and corporate responsibility, environmental awareness and local participation.

An organization's culture is therefore a repository of its principal beliefs and values. All of these beliefs and values are very powerful in affecting how an organization operates and how it responds to both internal events and external influences. In this way, culture provides a consistent basis for how an organization behaves. It has a positive contribution to holding the organization together and for moving it forward in its desired direction. Interestingly, however, a strong culture can also sometimes be a disadvantage, as it may slow down the organizational change that is sometimes necessary to ensure the organization's future survival.

Communicating business purpose

An organization's business purpose, culture, beliefs and values bind the organization together and provide individuals and groups with an overall rationale for their activities and actions. Some organizations take the development and communication of their business purpose very seriously, which can result in formal *mission statements* that define each element of this purpose in detail.

Such a formalized process and output may well be effective in some organizations, although in other cases it does appear that these organizations are merely going through the motions rather than being interested in providing some overall guidance. Thus, in some organizations, mission statements only seem to make their appearance in official documents and in corporate PR, rather than being seen in the actions and behaviour of the organization and its employees.

It is certainly of benefit to identify and record the principal aspects of an organization's business purpose and to document it in some way. However, the key issue is to find an effective way of translating business purpose into the realities of organizational life.

Perhaps a more effective way of developing and communicating a sense of purpose is by embedding its key elements into how leaders and managers behave and how they are seen to behave around the organization. This is the process that will be developed below. It makes the assumption that by focusing on the key elements of culture, leaders and managers can embed the principal elements of their business purpose into their organizations.

Much has been written about culture, but perhaps one of the most practical treatments of the subject was by Edgar Schein in his book, *Organizational Culture and Leadership*. In this book he suggests that there are certain mechanisms that managers use to create and reinforce culture.

Schein divided these elements into *primary mechanisms*, which are particularly important as organizations develop from their earliest beginnings, and *secondary mechanisms*, which become more important as the organizations mature. Taken together, both primary and secondary mechanisms are influential on the development and communication of culture around organizations. Figure 6.3 identifies all of these elements.

FIGURE 6.3   Culture-embedding mechanisms

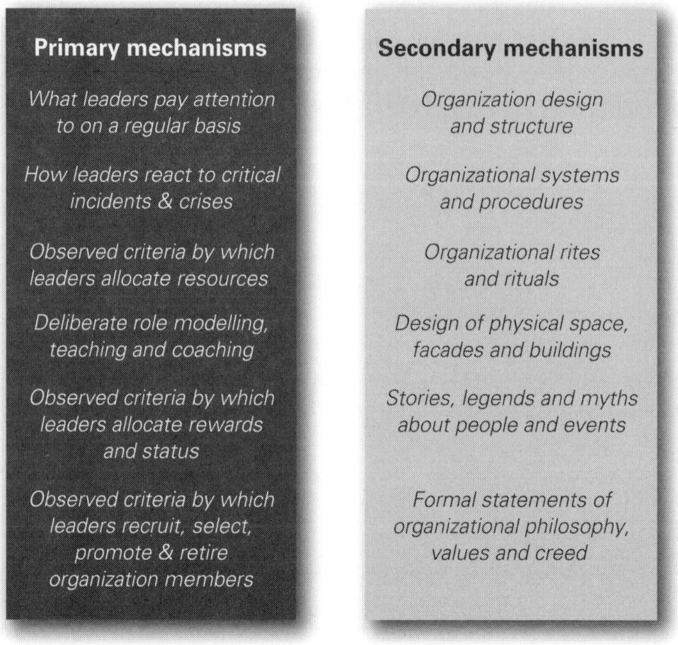

Primary mechanisms	Secondary mechanisms
What leaders pay attention to on a regular basis	Organization design and structure
How leaders react to critical incidents & crises	Organizational systems and procedures
Observed criteria by which leaders allocate resources	Organizational rites and rituals
Deliberate role modelling, teaching and coaching	Design of physical space, facades and buildings
Observed criteria by which leaders allocate rewards and status	Stories, legends and myths about people and events
Observed criteria by which leaders recruit, select, promote & retire organization members	Formal statements of organizational philosophy, values and creed

Primary mechanisms of culture

What leaders pay attention to on a regular basis

What leaders notice and pay attention to sends very strong signals to the whole organization and demonstrates in real terms what is considered to be most important. In addition to paying attention to key performance areas and other measurables, by observing and recognizing other aspects of organizational life, leaders have a very powerful influence on how an organization operates and behaves. The notion of *management by walking about* is based on the premise that leaders influence every aspect of their organization by what they pay attention to or notice.

Leaders who recognize the power of this personal influence are often very visible in the organization and can regularly be seen talking to staff from all departments. In department stores, for example, leaders will be regularly seen examining merchandising displays, paying attention to store cleanliness and picking up on the helpfulness and energy of staff. This degree of attention to detail will have more impact on organizational activity and behaviour than any number of words written into a mission statement.

Similarly, leaders of organizations at the forefront of innovation will spend most of their time talking to customers about their requirements and expectations, and then talking to designers about how these needs can be translated into new products. Such action will very clearly demonstrate the key aspects of business purpose that such leaders want to embed in their organization.

How leaders react to critical incidents and crises

A critical incident or crisis in the organization heightens the organization's awareness and sensitivity. It is during these periods that leadership actions are most closely scrutinized.

The saying 'When the going gets tough, the tough get going' fits very well in explaining this particular aspect of leadership. It is easy to do the right things when everything is calm and peaceful but much harder when problems or crises hit. Management can therefore display their true colours during such times of stress, and so their response to critical incidents is a particularly important signal to the organization of what is really important and worth defending.

For example, those organizations that hold product quality to be an essential aspect of their business purpose will be watched very closely when incidents put this aspect at risk. Organizations that truly believe in this element of their philosophy would rather withdraw their products from the market until the issue is resolved than compromise their quality reputation. As a further example, organizations that state a belief in employee involvement and participation will continue to share information about their future staffing levels and intentions even at times when economic conditions make changes to employee terms and conditions inevitable.

Observed criteria by which leaders allocate resources

The allocation of resources, which often comes down to money and budgets in most organizations, is a very clear signal of importance and intent. Therefore, how leaders behave in terms of committing money and budget to new products or to new ways of conducting business is a clear signal of essential values and beliefs. Time is also a scarce organizational resource, and so the giving of time for individuals or groups to pursue specific initiatives is another powerful way that leaders can demonstrate their commitment to certain aspects of their strategy and business purpose.

Deliberate role modelling, teaching and coaching

The behaviour of leaders is watched very closely by the rest of the organization. What they do, what they say and what they approve are minutely scrutinized and talked about. Leaders can therefore strongly affect their organization by demonstrating the kinds of activities and behaviours they wish to see copied by others.

Leaders who participate in customer negotiations or supplier meetings have recognized these important opportunities to display actions and behaviours that are in line with the core beliefs and values of the organization. Furthermore, by taking an active interest in teaching and coaching, leaders can directly communicate the key aspects of business purpose to the wider organization. This can be achieved by speaking at internal events and by taking an active part in recruitment, induction and training.

Observed criteria by which leaders allocate rewards and status

Rewards and status are probably two of the most important aspects of organizational life. Most aspects of individual and group behaviour are best explained by efforts to secure additional rewards and status.

Most people within organizations are acutely conscious of how rewards and status are allocated. Therefore, a leader's allocation of rewards and status will clearly demonstrate what is important and will also serve to encourage similar actions in the future. Sometimes, however, the allocation of rewards can conflict with stated business strategy, such as when sections of the organization are asked to work as a team and to pool resources, whilst rewards are still allocated on an individual basis. As we will consider in Chapter 8 on motivation, rewards are some of the principal tools that leaders use to encourage the actions and behaviours required for success.

Observed criteria by which leaders recruit, select, promote and retire organizational members

How leaders and managers behave in relation to these elements has a similar impact to that of rewards and status. The way that favour is bestowed on certain individuals, particularly the reasons for promotion, is a very clear indication of those actions and behaviours that are most highly regarded. This is a clear signal that such behaviour should be copied by others if they also value advancement and promotion.

Secondary mechanisms of culture

The following so-called *secondary mechanisms* tend to reinforce culture rather than create it in young organizations. However, as an organization matures, these elements become more important and can constrain management's attempts to make changes in an organization. These elements are listed below:

- organization design and structure;
- organizational systems and procedures;

- organizational rites and rituals;
- design of physical space, facades and buildings;
- stories, legends and myths about people and events;
- formal statements of organizational philosophy, values and creed.

These elements are self-explanatory and are probably the things that most people associate with the word culture. They tend to be more physical manifestations of the organization, or elements that can be more clearly observed and noticed. As such, they are probably more important in symbolizing culture than in actually creating it, and therefore are not as important as the other, more subtle but more powerful ways of creating culture that we have already looked at in this chapter.

All of the above elements of culture taken together shape and influence the whole internal organization. They also shape the way that the organization responds to its external competitive environment. For these reasons, culture is an important element in shaping sales and customer strategy and in creating business performance. The key question that emerges from the above discussion for managers and leaders is therefore: *How are you going to utilize the elements of culture to strengthen and reinforce your business purpose?*

Leadership

Hopefully this chapter has made the case for leadership and management in both the creation and communication of business purpose and in the creation of the culture that supports it. Given that we have previously identified a similar role in the creation of strategic direction, which began our investigation of sales and customer strategy in Part Two, it is clear that management creates the framework and environment for business success. This essential role will be explored in more detail in the remaining chapters of Part Two when we consider people, performance, development and motivation.

Leadership v management

We have tended to use the terms *leadership* and *management* interchangeably, but in reality they are quite different. Leadership takes a more strategic perspective, while management is more operational in nature. Of course, both of these complimentary aspects of behaviour are necessary, and often within small- to medium-sized organizations these behaviours will be displayed by one individual or within a small group of individuals who head up the organization.

Workshops and case studies

A number of workshops and case studies can be found below. These are designed to help the reader apply some of the techniques discussed in this chapter and to illustrate how organizations have coped with some of the issues involved.

WORKSHOP   Business Purpose Workshop 1:
Identifying business purpose and culture

Objective

This workshop is designed to identify the link between business purpose and culture and to formulate a strategy for strengthening culture in support of organizational objectives.

Process 1

Ask participants to examine Figure 6.2 and ask themselves which value delivery strategy is closest to explaining how the organization looks to compete in its usual marketplace.

Key questions

- Do you seek operational excellence?
- Do you look to achieve product leadership?
- Do you pursue customer intimacy?
- Do you pursue a reasonable mix of the above?
- Are you happy with this mix or does it suggest a lack of clarity?

Process 2

Staying with the same diagram, ask participants to now consider whether their *culture* supports the value delivery strategy.

Key questions

- Do you mainly follow process without deviation?
- Do you allow experimentation and creative thinking?
- Do you allow people great flexibility of action in support of customers?
- Is there a conflict between any of the elements?
- What do you want to change?

Process 3

Now ask participants to look at Figure 6.3 and select those elements that will help them make the changes required.

Key questions

- What do you need to spend more management attention on?

- How should you react to critical incidents and crises?

- How should you be seen to allocate resources, rewards and status?

- What areas should you be involved in when it comes to deliberate role modelling, teaching or coaching?

- What clear criteria should you use for recruitment, selection, promotion and retiring?

CASE STUDY   Business Purpose Case Study 1: Manufacturer of swimming pools and spas – Identifying key beliefs and values

Background

The company manufactures swimming pools for home owners and for larger residential complexes and hotels in the Gulf States. It wanted to develop a consistent management style across all of its regional offices that focused on its key values of customer service and after-sales in support of its unique product and service offering.

Activity

A facilitated management workshop was conducted with all key members of the management team from all regional offices. The structure of the workshop followed the approach taken in this chapter by first examining the organization's business purpose and business strategy to check for alignment. The particular culture-embedding mechanisms that required management attention were then identified.

Key learning points

- This workshop was the first time that all key members of the organization had met to discuss these issues. They all felt that it had been extremely valuable to understand the range of thoughts that existed among these individuals.

- Some uncomfortable truths were tabled during the meeting, particularly around the variations in management style and how information was communicated around the organization.

- All agreed to a consistent style of management in all day-to-day management activities in order to communicate a common set of beliefs and values.

- A programme of change was instigated with key members of the management team given responsibility for addressing particular concerns.

CASE STUDY   Business Purpose Case Study 2: Provider of market intelligence – Recognizing and rewarding organizational values

Background

The company provides a market intelligence and media scanning service to its clients. It had undertaken previous work in workshops to identify its core competencies, market definition and competitive positioning. It now wanted to build on this work in order to recognize and reward behaviour in line with its core values of customer service and professional response.

Activity

The strategic direction that had earlier been defined for the organization was translated into a range of required activities and behaviours for every individual with a customer-facing role. These behaviours were designed to embody the key values and the belief that professional customer service was the key element of competitive strategy for the organization.

Key learning points

- Managers realized that irrespective of what they said was important, it was what they were seen to recognize and reward that really made the difference to organizational behaviour.

- Managers also realized that it was not just the final end results that should be recognized, but also those activities and behaviours that often went unnoticed but were equally important in transmitting the required level of service to customers.

- The incentive and reward scheme was therefore changed to also reward behaviours that supported the organization's overall strategy and key values. Management made the giving of these rewards highly visible around the organization.

People and performance
What should our people be able to do?

07

FIGURE 7.1 The Business Performance Value Chain:
People and Performance

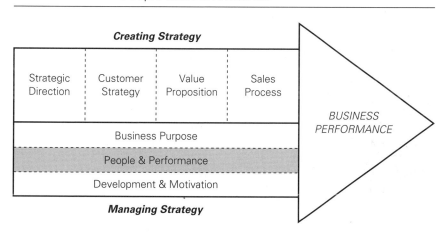

In this chapter we look at the structure of the organization and how this should be designed to accommodate the sales and customer strategy. The roles of individuals within this structure will also be considered.

We will then examine the *performance management framework* that identifies the essential levers of management control responsible for creating organizational performance. In particular, we will examine the difference between the *key performance measures* (the *ends*) and those elements that create this performance (the *means*).

People

Organizational theory suggests that *structure follows strategy*. This implies an essential link between the strategy to be delivered and the structure needed to deliver it. This might sound obvious, but it is not unusual to find organizations where this essential connection has not been made. In the worst of cases, the organization's structure makes it almost impossible to implement its strategy.

This lack of connection between strategy and structure is usually the result of how most organizations have evolved over time. They have normally grown in response to short-term competitive issues or as a result of internal politics, rather than in response to the needs of the sales and customer strategy.

The strategy of the business should define the type of people needed in the numbers that it needs them. It also defines how people should work together towards a common goal and objectives. Given that this book is focused on sales and customer strategy in B2B markets, and particularly on the winning and keeping of customers, the sales roles and sales structure needed should be derived directly from the sales strategy, as Figure 7.2 demonstrates.

FIGURE 7.2   Sales strategy/sales structure

Sales Strategy	*Finding*	*Engaging*	*Proving*	*Winning*	*Keeping*
	Searching / Prospecting	*Opening*	*Features / Benefits*	*Trading Value*	*Customer Satisfaction*
	Qualifying / Profiling	*Analysis / Fact Find*	*Value Proposition*	*Negotiation*	*Relationship Development*
	Targeting	*Summary & Vision*	*Evidence*	*Objection Handling*	*Added Value*

Sales Structure
Number & Type of Salespeople
Customer Portfolios
Account Teams
Targets & Territories

It can also be said that in B2B organizations, the overall sales strategy should not only inform the structure of the sales organization, but it should also do the same for the rest of the organization. In this way, the sales strategy can also be said to provide the *Organizational Blueprint* for the whole organization. We will look at this wider aspect of organizational structure later in the chapter.

Structure

The sales process is designed to engage with customers in the most effective way by responding to customer importance, the type of relationship customers require, and the customer buying process. The number and type of salespeople will therefore be defined by what the sales process requires them to do.

Going back to the Customer Relationship Matrix from Chapter 3 on customer strategy:

- If customers require a *transactional relationship*, then a cost-effective way of serving these customers without the intervention of a direct sales force should be developed.

- If customers require a *negotiated relationship*, then very commercial salespeople who are good deal-makers are needed.

- If customers require a *consultative relationship*, then highly qualified technical salespeople or highly qualified professionals are needed.

- If customers require a *collaborative relationship*, then all-round business professionals capable of working at the highest level are needed.

Management must then decide if the sales process to manage customers through every stage of their buying process requires account planning or activity management. This will depend on the numbers of customers being managed and the complexity of the buying process.

Account planning is implied where there are a relatively small number of customers with complex buying processes, whereas *activity management* is implied where there are a relatively large number of smaller customers with relatively simple buying processes. Most organizations find that they need a combination of both, with some customers requiring account planning and others requiring activity management. This has an impact on the type of salespeople needed.

Number and type of salespeople

The analysis of your customers may require a number of roles as shown in Figure 7.3.

FIGURE 7.3   Customer management structures

KAM	Key Account Manager
AM	Account Manager
AE	Account Executive
TAM	Telephone Account Manager

Key account manager (KAM)

Key account managers look after the most important customers. These customers are either *key accounts* that provide most of the organization's current business, or *development accounts* that represent the best opportunities for new business.

Key account managers will have all the basic sales skills, but will also have higher-level abilities, such as:

- the ability to develop effective relationships at all levels in the customer organization;
- the ability to manage their own organization to win resources for their customers;
- the ability to create account plans that identify opportunities and to create account strategy to realize them;
- industry knowledge, financial awareness, marketing techniques and higher-level personal and communication skills.

Key account managers will often have a small number of customers, as these customers deserve considerable attention and focus. Key account managers spend most of their time with their customers on their premises and will only be seen around the organization when attending account strategy meetings or if they are trying to organize specific initiatives for their customers.

Account manager (AM)

Account managers fulfil a similar role to key account managers, although they normally manage the next tier of customers below the key accounts. They usually manage more customers than key account managers because these customers have not yet grown to the point where they are considered key accounts or development accounts, although they do have the potential to achieve this status over time.

Account managers are often key account managers in development, in that they are seen to have the potential to become key account managers and to manage the organization's most important customers in the future. Account managers will also spend much of their time with customers, rather than being seen around the office.

Account executive (AE)

Account executives are normally office based and manage the next tier of customers below those managed by the account managers. They manage a much greater number of customers than the account managers do. Much of their work is therefore conducted over the telephone or by other means, with customers that probably do not have the potential to grow into key accounts or development accounts.

Telephone account executive (TAE)

Telephone account executives handle the largest number of customers and are normally office based. They manage the next tier of customers below those managed by the account executives. These customers only require a transactional relationship, which can either be delivered over the telephone or by some other means.

Customer portfolios

Allocating customers to the appropriate level of account manager or account executive is not an exact science. Historically the criterion used has been historical revenue, but this simple classification does not take into account other important factors such as future business potential, the strategic importance of the account, its risk of being lost to competitors, or its level of complexity.

Given that it is not straightforward to allocate customers to the appropriate level of account handler, the practice of creating fixed customer portfolios for each level of account handler exacerbates the problem by not allowing customers to effectively find their own level of customer management. A better practice is to create some flexibility that allows customers to be handled in the most appropriate way by the most appropriate level of account handler.

This flexibility can be provided if team targets are adopted that encourage individuals to share opportunities and to share the management of customers, rather than to keep them for themselves. This issue is explored in Case Study 1 at the end of this chapter.

Account teams

The importance of account teams has grown in recent years to reflect the need to manage larger customers that sometimes span wide geographical areas or even countries. Account teams or groups of salespeople working together on a shared number of customers must address a range of issues, typically:

- What constitutes a global account?
- How should the account team be constituted?

- Who manages the account team and what should its reporting relationships be?
- How should sales revenues be allocated across the global organization?
- How should the account team be resourced (management, funding, operations, logistics) across national boundaries?

The political aspects of putting together such teams should not be under-estimated, as they typically cut across national organizations that have up to this point enjoyed their own independence and autonomy.

This use of account teams raises a more general point about the use of teamwork in sales. The sales role is often seen as a solitary role, with sales-people largely working in splendid isolation. This is true up to a point, but the notion of a team approach within sales is also important for the following reasons:

- the sharing of customer information and market intelligence;
- the sharing of best practice;
- the allocation of customer opportunities to the most appropriate salesperson;
- the provision of opportunities for social interaction and support;
- the option to allocate specific roles based on particular skills;
- the opportunity to provide for increased responsibility and development.

There are therefore a number of good reasons to generate an overall team approach within sales. This aspect is looked at in greater detail in Chapter 8 on development.

Targets and territories

Targets and territories are another important aspect of sales structure. The objective of creating targets and territories is to allocate specific responsibility for achieving a part of the total sales task to individuals with their own customers contained within a geographical area.

However, in many sales organizations the sales targets and territories are seen to be unfair, as they do not reflect the realistic sales potential and opportunity offered by either the number of accounts in question or the potential of the geographical area. Typically, this is due to an over-reliance on historical sales performance rather than on a realistic analysis of sales potential.

Targets and territories should therefore be designed to reflect actual sales potential and provide an equal chance of sales success across territories. See Case Study 2 at the end of this chapter.

The Organizational Blueprint

We have discussed the fact that structure follows strategy and related this to the sales organization. This same principle applies to the rest of the organization.

If it is assumed that for commercial organizations, the most fundamental aspect of strategy is to win and keep customers, then it follows that sales and customer strategy should create the overall rationale or Organizational Blueprint for the whole organization. This is represented in Figure 7.4.

FIGURE 7.4 Organizational Blueprint

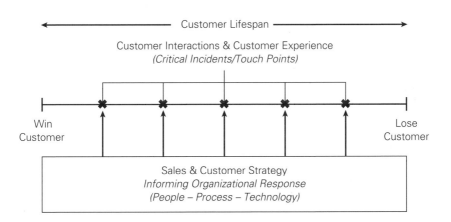

Customer lifespan

Customers have a lifespan. They are won, they stay with the organization for a period of time, and then they can be lost either to competition or to the ravages of commercial evolution.

Customer interactions

During this customer lifespan, a number of *customer interactions* occur. These interactions can also be referred to as *critical incidents* or *customer touch-points*.

For B2C organizations, these customer interactions can run into many thousands every day, whereas this number of interactions is normally much smaller for those organizations operating in B2B. These interactions can take many forms, including: *enquiries, information requests, ordering, order status enquiries, billing, customer service requests* and *complaints*.

The first task in arriving at an Organizational Blueprint is to identify and map these typical customer interactions for the typical lifespan of a customer. This should describe in detail what happens during each customer interaction.

The customer experience

Having identified these customer touch-points or critical incidents, which can of course have either a positive or a negative connotation, the next stage of the process is to define the ideal *customer experience* that the organization wants to create at each touch-point. This experience relates to the ideal physical or emotional impact that the customer experiences when he or she engages with the organization at each touch-point. Having established the ideal experience, it is a useful exercise to measure the actual experience that customers report when dealing with the organization.

Organizational response

Any gap between the *ideal* and the *existing* customer experience should be analysed to establish the changes that need to be made to improve the situation. These changes could have implications for every aspect of the organization's activities that are covered under the broad headings of *people*, *process* and *technology*, not just on aspects that are traditionally customer facing (see Case Study 2 at the end of this chapter).

Performance

Performance is all about delivering the goods. It's about achieving objectives and hitting the numbers. This is certainly true, but how can this level of success be achieved?

In order for performance to be created, something has to be done to produce it. Performance therefore has two major components: what you put in (inputs) versus what you get out (outputs).

This is a discussion about *ends* and *means*. The *ends* are the levels of performance that the organization is looking to achieve, and the *means* relate to what is required to get this result.

This is one of the fundamental principles of performance, which states that if you do the right things, the right things will happen. Outstanding performance is no accident. Outstanding sales performance can sometimes be a question of luck, but generally there must be something else going on. Good salespeople are like good sportspeople; they must be doing the right things most of the time.

Let's look at a football analogy. Would a football manager help their team to win matches by shouting 'Score more goals!' from the touchline? If you were Sir Alex Ferguson (the 'Hairdryer') you might get away with this for a while, but for the rest of us, this management approach probably would not be very successful.

Scoring more goals is surely a good objective, but merely shouting that from the touchline does not give any idea of how this might be achieved. Likewise, in sales, too much management activity is concentrated on the end result, with an over-emphasis on the target itself rather than on what actions will get the target achieved.

If we take the football analogy further, the football manager needs to work very hard in training on coaching their team to shut down opponents quickly, to provide good chances for the forwards, and to ensure these chances are put away. There is therefore a belief that by transferring these skills onto the pitch on match-day, *we will* score more goals and *we will* be more successful.

Likewise for the sales manager. Rather than screaming 'Hit those targets!' from the sidelines, he or she should coach salespeople to better understand customer needs, to formulate good business propositions and to make attractive presentations that win customer support. Thus, by transferring these skills into the sales environment, there is a belief that *we will* get more of the customers' business and *we will* be successful as a result.

So, to answer the question posed earlier, although business is all about hitting objectives and doing the numbers, the focus of management attention should also be on the development of those actions and behaviours that lead to sales success.

Controlling performance: The sales performance framework

The sales performance framework shown in Figure 7.5 can be used to help identify all the elements of performance, and then define how they can be measured, monitored and managed.

FIGURE 7.5   The sales performance framework

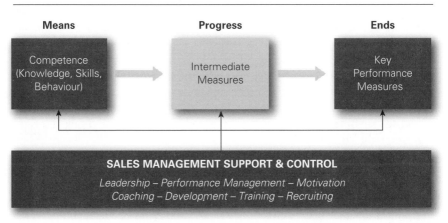

This approach is the essence of performance management: *having appropriate measures of the key levers of sales performance and the knowledge of how to intervene in order to make a positive difference.* In this section we will therefore explore sales performance in detail to establish the appropriate control measures by which each element of performance can be managed. Later, in Chapter 8 on development and motivation, we will look at how sales performance can be improved and even transformed.

Key performance measures – the ends

The achievement of key performance measures (also known as *key result areas* or *key measures of success*) are the *ends* to be aimed for and constitute the ultimate measures of success. They include:

- sales targets;
- sales volume;

- sales value;
- profit margin;
- total amount of profit;
- proportion of new business generated;
- number of new accounts opened;
- customer satisfaction;
- customer retention.

Performance management and key performance measures

The key performance measures are rightly a focus of management attention and are usually monitored by the creation of appropriate targets. Results are therefore compared against objectives and any discrepancy is investigated and hopefully corrected. This is the principle of management by exception.

Intermediate performance measures – progress

Management often focuses its entire attention on key performance measures without giving sufficient attention to how this performance is achieved. When managing performance, measures are also needed that provide reassurance that adequate progress towards these key performance measures is being made. These are called *intermediate performance measures*, and they allow assessment of the progress made towards ultimate success. There are three main ways in which managers can monitor and measure intermediate performance, as outlined below.

'Chunked-down' goals

One way to measure intermediate progress against key performance measures is to break them down into bite-sized chunks. A typical way of doing this is to divide an annual objective into 12 monthly targets. As we will discuss in Chapter 8 on motivation, breaking down objectives into bite-sized chunks is also an important means of creating a momentum of success.

Activity management

Activity management provides opportunities to measure progress towards key performance measures. Although we looked at activity management in *Customer Strategy*, we will look at it again as an intermediate performance measure. In activity management, salespeople are dealing with a large number

FIGURE 7.6   Activity management: The sales funnel

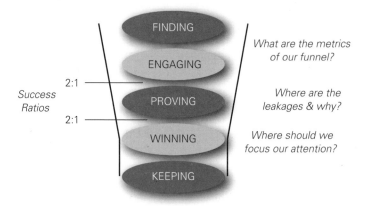

of smaller accounts and the sales funnel provides a way of monitoring and measuring intermediate performance (see Figure 7.6). The sales funnel allows managers to measure the following:

- the number of leads being produced that enter the top of the funnel (finding);
- the number of leads that result in sales meetings (engaging);
- the number of sales meetings that result in a proposal being presented (proving);
- the number of proposals that result in a sale (winning).
- the number of customers retained (keeping).

The sales funnel therefore provides an early-warning system to indicate whether there are enough leads being produced, enough sales meetings taking place, enough proposals being presented, and enough customers being closed. Managers can set their own standards for these ratios in order to monitor intermediate progress against objectives. They can also be used as a comparison measure across the sales team.

A further way of measuring intermediate progress is by using some of the more traditional sales performance measures, such as:

- *Call rate* – the number of sales calls made in a particular period, such as daily or weekly.
- *Strike rate* – the ratio of calls where an order is taken to total sales calls.
- *Order size* – the total size of the order placed or the range of different products sold per customer order.

Key account planning

Key account planning can also be used to create intermediate performance measures. In key account management, the achievement of an overall goal may take a significant amount of time, so the only way to measure progress towards this goal is to use a key account plan and break the goal down into a series of individual objectives. The achievement of these objectives will therefore indicate whether progress towards the overall goal is being made.

FIGURE 7.7 Key account planning

These objectives can be part of any strategy that comes within the typical sales process stages of engaging, proving, winning or keeping. They could therefore include:

- formulation of an entry strategy;
- identifying the decision-making unit;
- finding a coach or sponsor.

Performance management and intermediate performance measures

Breaking goals down into smaller objectives and the use of activity management and key account planning are all ways that management can focus on intermediate measures of performance to ensure that progress is being made towards the key performance measures.

Competence – the means

Using the sales performance framework, we have now defined how to evaluate performance in two key areas: *intermediate measures of performance* and *key performance measures*. We can therefore measure whether progress is

FIGURE 7.8   Sales structure/sales competencies

Sales Process	Finding	Engaging	Proving	Winning	Keeping
	Searching	Opening	Features / Benefits	Objection Handling	Customer Satisfaction
	Prospecting	Analysis / Fact Find	Value Proposition	Trading Value	Relationship Development
	Qualifying	Summary & Vision	Evidence	Negotiation	Added Value

Sales Structure

Number & Type of Salespeople

Customer Portfolios

Account Teams

Targets & Territories

Sales competencies

Prospecting & Qualifying

Developing Credibility & Relationships

Identifying Customer Issues & Opportunities

Presenting Value Propositions

Negotiating & Closing

Managing the Sales Process

Territory & Time Management

being made towards the ultimate sales objectives and can also measure their final achievement.

We now need a way to measure whether there are the *means* to achieve the performance targets. This 'means' is provided by the ability of the salespeople to deliver what is required of the sales process, and this ability is measured by their competence in performing specific aspects of their role.

Sales competencies are therefore the capabilities that salespeople need in order to be successful. They are determined by the *sales process* and *sales structure* as outlined in Figure 7.8.

Competencies are things that people can do. They are broadly-based descriptions of overall capabilities. In sales terms, the ability to present value propositions is one such competence, and one that is closely linked with sales performance.

There are other competencies that are particularly important and are more likely to result in outstanding sales performance. These are referred to as *differentiating competencies*, as they are those capabilities that separate the good sales performers from the less good. For example, if you were to observe the good sales performers in action, you would be more likely to spot these competencies being demonstrated than would be the case when observing the less good sales performers.

FIGURE 7.9   Key sales competencies

> *Prospecting & Qualifying*
>
> *Developing Credibility & Relationships*
>
> *Identifying Customer Situation & Opportunities*
>
> *Presenting Value Propositions*
>
> *Obtaining Customer Commitment*
>
> *Managing Sales Process*
>
> *Territory & Time Management*

Ideally, an organization wants all of its salespeople to have these special capabilities that impact on sales performance. Therefore, the organization needs to know what these specific competencies are that create success in its particular sales environment.

Figure 7.9 lists some of the characteristic *competencies* required of a typical salesperson. This is of course a generic list of competencies that would apply to any typical sales situation. Each sales organization needs to develop its own list that relates to its own specific sales environment.

These typical sales competencies are defined below.

Prospecting and qualifying

Effective salespeople are good at prospecting and qualifying. They seem to be very successful in digging around their territories and sniffing out good prospects. They also seem to have a nose for those leads or suspects that are more likely to develop into business, and can be quite ruthless in deciding early on that certain leads are not likely to go anywhere.

Less effective salespeople spend more of their time chasing leads that don't go anywhere. They just seem to have fewer good prospects on the go at any particular time.

Developing credibility and relationships

Effective salespeople are good at developing credibility with customers and forming strong relationships. They are trusted by their customers, who value the support and advice they receive.

Less effective salespeople are not as successful in forming strong business relationships with their customers. They don't seem to enjoy the same trust and credibility that the best salespeople benefit from.

Identifying customer situation and opportunities

Effective salespeople are good at identifying the decision-making process and the decision-making unit of their customers. They are also good at identifying customer issues, concerns and opportunities. They can turn the problems of their customers into business opportunities and always seem to be in the right place at the right time.

Less effective salespeople are not as good at identifying the customer's situation or understanding their true requirements and expectations. As a result, they are less successful at turning customer problems into opportunities.

Presenting value propositions

Good salespeople can develop propositions that create maximum value for their customers. They are also skilled at communicating their customer value propositions in an interesting and effective way.

Less successful salespeople are not always able to develop propositions that demonstrate customer value. As a result, their presentations are not as effective in generating customer interest.

Obtaining customer commitment

Effective salespeople always seem able to move customers forward towards a particular course of action and are very skilled at winning business. Less effective salespeople are less likely to win customer commitment towards a course of action and are not as good at winning business.

Managing the sales process

Successful salespeople seem to have a clear idea of their customer's buying process and of their customer's current position within it. They also seem to know what their customers will do next and are therefore rarely caught by surprise by anything the customer might do.

Less effective salespeople, on the other hand, are often unclear about their customer's position in the buying process. They are often surprised and wrong-footed by a customer's unexpected actions.

Territory and time management

Effective salespeople are good managers of their time and their territories. They seem to extract the last ounce of potential from their customers and always devote their time to important activities.

Less successful salespeople often seem to waste time on unproductive tasks. They don't often seem able to extract the full potential from their customers and territories.

Knowledge, skills and behaviour

By identifying the competencies that salespeople must have in order to be successful, we have made an excellent start in understanding how sales performance is created as part of the sales performance framework. But we need to go further; we need to identify how these competencies came about, and what their constituent parts are.

The competencies described above are themselves made up of a combination of more fundamental personal attributes, namely *knowledge*, *skills* and *behaviours*. These are the building blocks of those sales competencies that lead to sales performance and sales success.

Competence = knowledge + skill + behaviour

As an example, the competence *identifying customer situation and opportunities* is made possible by *knowledge* of the industry, the customer and the organization's own proposition, together with the *skills* of questioning and probing, and the *behaviours* of tenacity and desire. We therefore need to drill down to the essential constituents of each competence to identify what they are made from.

Figure 7.10 identifies the typical knowledge, skills and behaviours that are normally required for effective sales performance. These are the building blocks of the key competencies defined earlier.

Each competence therefore brings together a particular mix of knowledge, skills and behaviour.

FIGURE 7.10   Key sales attributes

Knowledge	Skill	Behaviour
	Listening	Professionalism
Market Environment	Questioning & Probing	Commitment
		Initiative
Company Proposition	Communicating & Presenting	Tenacity
Competitive Positioning	Trading Value & Negotiating	Self-motivation
		Diligence
Company Procedures	Closing	Desire
	Analysing & Planning	Energy & Enthusiasm

The constituent elements of each competence are identified below.

TABLE 7.1   Competence: Prospecting and qualifying

Knowledge	Skill	Behaviour
Territory	Questioning	Tenacity
Customer	Analysing/planning	Desire

TABLE 7.2   Competence: Developing credibility and relationships

Knowledge	Skill	Behaviour
Propositions	Questioning	Professionalism
Industry/customer	Probing	

TABLE 7.3   Competence: Identifying customer situation/ opportunities

Knowledge	Skill	Behaviour
Propositions	Questioning	Tenacity
Industry/customer	Probing	Desire

TABLE 7.4   Competence: Presenting value propositions

Knowledge	Skill	Behaviour
Customer	Communicating	Professionalism
	Presenting	

TABLE 7.5 Competence: Obtaining customer commitment

Knowledge	Skill	Behaviour
Customer	Negotiating	Persistence
	Objection handling	Desire

TABLE 7.6 Competence: Managing sales process

Knowledge	Skill	Behaviour
Sales process	Analysing	Desire
Customer DMU/DMP	Planning	Self-motivation

TABLE 7.7 Competence: Territory and time management

Knowledge	Skill	Behaviour
Customer	Analysing	Self-motivation
Territory	Planning	Desire

Standards of performance

Having defined the key sales competencies and the knowledge, skills and behaviours that form them, we now need to define the level of performance required in each of these elements in order to determine if a salesperson is being effective. We must therefore define standards of performance for those competencies that set the required level of performance expected from all salespeople.

Competency profiles

The development of competencies and standards of performance expected from salespeople ensure that the factors that lead to sales performance can be measured and assessed. A competency profile can therefore be developed that brings together all the competencies and standards of performance into a single document.

The competency profile is designed to be used by the management when observing the performance of salespeople in field appraisal. It is therefore an important tool for monitoring and measuring the means by which sales performance is created, and forms an essential part of the manager's performance management toolkit. Assessment of salespeople against this competency profile will also influence training and development across the sales organization.

Performance management summary

The sales performance framework defines how management control and support sales performance on a number of different levels to create the overall environment for sales success. It does this by creating the relevant performance measures to monitor and control the *means*, the *progress* and the *ends* of sales performance.

Regular measures of performance and comparison against objectives, intermediate measures and other standards of performance are therefore an important part of management activity. Appropriate management action is then taken to bring performance back to its expected level.

Much of the insight into those factors that create sales performance will also be useful in developing a *job specification* for any particular sales role. This job specification specifies exactly what the role consists of and what is expected of it. The following section shows an example of how to create a competency profile and job description for an account manager.

Example competency profile: Account manager

Background information

Account managers are responsible for all customers in a geographical area. They have a mixture of existing accounts (30–40 each) but are also targeted to win new customers. They are also targeted against customer satisfaction measures provided by customers.

Approximately six customers will require account planning and the rest will be *managed via activity management*. Account managers also have to work as a team with internally based telephone account managers who have their own portfolio of around 200 customers. This sometimes necessitates account managers making sales calls to support their colleagues.

There are eight account managers in the business, who are geographically spread around the country. Out of these eight managers, there is one star performer who generates the highest levels of business from existing and new accounts. There are two more managers who are very good, three that seem to be fairly middling, and two who are not performing well, with one of them struggling to make the grade.

Customer buying process/sales process

Table 7.8 outlines the *customer buying process* and the matching *sales process* required of the account managers (see Chapter 5 on the sales process). The customer buying process was developed through detailed knowledge of how these particular customers make buying decisions and who is typically involved at each stage. The sales process was an agreed response to this buying process, identifying the necessary sales actions. It is therefore this

TABLE 7.8 Customer buying process and sales process

Customer buying process	Sales process
NEED & SEARCH	FIND & ENGAGE
Understand issues/needs	Generate leads
Look for potential suppliers	Qualify prospect
	Initial approach
Agree selection criteria	Identify customer issues
	Identify important customer personnel
EVALUATION	PROVING
Assess suppliers	Develop business proposition
	Present customer proposition
DECISION	WINNING
	Address issues and concerns
Negotiate best deal	Manage contract negotiations
REVIEW	KEEPING
Ensure investment works	Manage first use/installation
Monitor reliability/after-sales response	Manage after-sales response
Further purchase	Identify further opportunities
	Use sale as reference site

sales process, with its implications for the activities of the account manager, that will provide the framework for observations and further discussions.

Steps for developing the competency profile

- Step 1: Key performance measures and intermediate performance measures
- Step 2: Observation of activities and behaviours
- Step 3: Codification of observations into competencies and sales attributes
- Step 4: Development of performance standards and how performance is monitored and measured

Step 1: Key performance measures and intermediate performance measures

In this example, the key measures of success and the intermediate performance measures for the account managers are as follows.

Sales targets

- 100 per cent of sales volume target;
- 25 per cent of which must be from new customers;
- stretch target amounting to 120 per cent of sales target also set;
- gross profit margin of 33 per cent required on all sales;
- customer satisfaction required to be 75 percent.

Intermediate performance measures

- Account plans for the six customers being managed with account plans.
- Activity management measures for the remaining customers.

Step 2: Observation of activities and behaviours

Over the last three months, two days have been spent with each account manager to observe them in action and discuss their attitudes to certain aspects of their job. At the same time, the opportunity was used to discuss what these salespeople liked and disliked about their role and what they liked doing outside of work. This was intended to help identify particular motivators and demotivators for each individual (discussed further in Chapter 8 on motivation).

The observations identified a range of activities and behaviours from the good and less good performers as outlined in Table 7.9.

TABLE 7.9   Observed actions and behaviours

Good performers	Less good performers
Ability to develop good personal and business relationships	Good personal relationships but not developing into business relationships
Ability to identify best prospects from leads	Seem to follow up all leads in the same way
Good knowledge of industry issues and ability to relate them to customers' business	Fair knowledge of industry issues but not good at relating them to customers' business
Good knowledge of customer situation, particularly their issue and requirements in order of priority	Good knowledge of issues, but unsure of their priority
Good knowledge of all customer decision makers, influencers and potential sponsors	Incomplete knowledge, particularly of influencers and sponsors
Understanding of which customers are most important – reflected in customer priorities	No notion of customer importance or priorities
Good at networking around the customer to find out issues and opportunities	Restricted access to customer with little evidence of networking
Good at listening and giving positive customer feedback	Sometimes seems to plough on with own agenda rather than listening to customer
Good presenter and communicator, able to hold attention and interest	Sometimes a bit rambling and unstructured, on occasion losing customers' interest
Good at winning customer business through objection handling, negotiation and trading value	Not always able to win business – often poor at handling objections and trading value

TABLE 7.9   *continued*

Good performers	Less good performers
Good at relating product and service benefits to specific customer needs	Sometimes guilty of giving set spiel even though customer issues and needs require specific input
Very credible and professional in the eyes of the customer	Sometimes seen as lacking credibility
Enthusiastic and motivated, which communicates itself to customers	Sometimes comes across as lacklustre and just going through the motions
Plan and strategy for each customer; always knew what they were trying to achieve at every contact	Unsure of customer objectives with some actions seeming arbitrary and aimless
Good at winning internal support and resources for customer activities	Struggles to obtain internal support
Very open to feedback and positive criticism	Very resistant to criticism and feedback
Keen to develop and progress	No real ambition to develop and progress
Keen to attend training programmes	Will attend training programmes but appears uncommitted
Prompt and accurate responses to demands for information	Often unresponsive and late with information
Positive and enthusiastic at sales meetings	Attends sales meetings but sometimes negative
Often generating improvement ideas	Never produces any ideas
Alive to opportunities	Seem to miss opportunities
Good knowledge of company's product and service offering	Incomplete knowledge of company's product and service offering

Step 3: Codification of observations into competencies and sales attributes

Having observed the range of activities and behaviours exhibited by the eight account managers, these must now be codified into a list of competencies and attributes (knowledge, skills and behaviours). This is done by examining each element of the observation and deciding what category it should come under.

Most are self-explanatory, but some may require a little more consideration. Some may also be repeated, but as long as each one is captured, this does not matter. Additionally, there may be some competencies identified that are specific to the role in question and do not appear on the generic lists shown above.

Competencies

- developing credibility and relationships;
- prospecting and qualifying;
- identifying customer situation and opportunities;
- internal and external networking (a competence specific to the role);
- winning business.

Key sales attributes

Knowledge:

- industry knowledge;
- customer knowledge;
- company knowledge.

Skill:

- listening;
- communicating;
- presenting;
- planning and organizing.

Behaviour:

- energy and enthusiasm;
- initiative;
- professionalism;
- self-motivation.

Step 4: Development of performance standards and how performance is monitored and measured

We are now in a position to complete the competency profile for those competencies that create successful performance in an account manager.

We need to produce definitions of those behaviours or actions that will indicate the presence or otherwise of each particular competence or key sales attribute. These standards of performance should be:

- understood;
- observable;
- measurable.

It is useful to develop a range of standards, in this case three standards that span the spectrum of performance:

- below standard;
- required standard;
- above standard.

This provides the opportunity to recognize over-performance.

Example of a performance standard for a competence

As was stated earlier, competencies are things that people can do. They are broadly based descriptions of overall capabilities. The example that will be used is *managing the sales process.*

Competence: *Managing the sales process*
Definition: *The ability to retain control of the sales process in order to guide the customer towards a successful conclusion.*

TABLE 7.10   Managing the sales process performance standard

Performance standard	Performance definition
Above standard	Outstanding ability to manage the sales process and guide the customer towards a successful conclusion
Required standard	Mostly able to manage the sales process and guide the customer towards a successful conclusion
Below standard	Not often able to manage the sales process and guide the customer towards a successful conclusion

A similar process is then repeated for all the competencies identified.

Example of a performance standard for knowledge

Defining knowledge is relatively easy as it normally refers to knowledge of the industry, the customer and the salesperson's own organization. Let's use *customer knowledge* as an example.

Knowledge: Customer knowledge
Definition: *The ability to understand the customer's situation, particularly their needs and expectations.*

TABLE 7.11 Customer knowledge performance standard

Performance standard	Performance definition
Above standard	Outstanding ability to identify the customer's situation, particularly their needs and expectations
Required standard	Mostly able to identify the customer's situation, particularly their needs and expectations
Below standard	Not often able to identify the customer's situation, particularly their needs and expectations

Example of a performance standard for a skill

Defining a skill is also relatively easy. Let's use listening as an example.

Skill: Listening
Definition: *The ability to hear and understand what the customer is saying and to acknowledge this understanding.*

TABLE 7.12 Listening performance standard

Performance standard	Performance definition
Above standard	Outstanding ability to hear and understand what the customer is saying and to acknowledge this understanding
Required standard	Mostly able to hear and understand what the customer is saying and to acknowledge this understanding
Below standard	Not often able to hear and understand what the customer is saying and to acknowledge this understanding

Example of a performance standard for a behaviour

Behaviour is the last attribute to be measured. We are focusing on behaviour rather than attitude because it is performance that we are ultimately interested in, and behaviours are easier to measure and more relevant to performance. For the example, let's look at professionalism.

Behaviour: Professionalism
Definition: The ability to demonstrate high levels of personal and professional standards.

TABLE 7.13 Professionalism performance standard

Performance standard	Performance definition
Above standard	Outstanding ability to demonstrate high levels of personal and professional standards
Required standard	Mostly able to demonstrate high levels of personal and professional standards
Below standard	Not often able to demonstrate high levels of personal and professional standards

How performance is monitored and measured

Account managers will be assessed on their performance as follows.

Key performance measures

- Achievement against sales targets will be assessed on a monthly basis.
- Incentives will be paid quarterly according to performance.
- Customer satisfaction will be assessed quarterly.

Intermediate measures of performance

- Account plans will be discussed monthly and appropriate account strategies agreed.
- Activity management results will be assessed monthly.

Competencies

Account managers will also be appraised using the field appraisal document every 4–6 weeks and their personal development plan adjusted accordingly.

Note: See Appendix 2 on page 168 for the field appraisal and Chapter 8 on development for the personal development plan.

Summary

The role of an account manager has been identified and details of how their performance will be monitored and assessed have been provided. In particular, the key performance measures on which the sales performance of account managers will ultimately be judged have been defined.

The requirements of the *sales process*, together with the observations carried out and knowledge of the role, have led to identification of a range of key competencies that are necessary for an account manager to be effective. The knowledge, skills and behaviours that constitute these competencies have also been identified, and certain actions and behaviours that demonstrate whether these competencies and attributes exist have been defined. These have been called the *standards of performance*.

Thus, a competency profile for an account manager that defines all standards of performance in ways that are observable and measurable has been created. In this way, management attention can ultimately be focused on developing those competencies that have the biggest impact on performance.

The manager now has the tools by which to measure and control performance and the important levers for creating the right culture of success. Management therefore now have crucial information available by which to measure and improve performance, rather than just shouting from the sidelines. When motivation and development are discussed in the next chapter, we will have all the levers of performance at our disposal.

This information can now be used in both a job description and a field appraisal document. See the appendices at the end of the chapter for examples.

Workshops and case studies

A number of workshops and case studies can be found below, designed to help the reader apply some of the techniques discussed in this chapter and to illustrate how organizations have coped with some of the issues raised.

WORKSHOP   People and Performance Workshop 1:
Developing terms of engagement

Objective

This workshop is designed to develop an understanding between managers and salespeople about what is expected from both parties in the relationship. These are the terms of engagement. The objective is to make sure that any potential issues or misunderstandings are cleared up early on in the relationship, to enable both parties to feel comfortable and confident in their role.

Process

This exercise does not re-examine the key performance measures of targets and objectives, but other aspects of the working relationship between the two parties.

1   Ask managers to write down what they expect from their salespeople in the following areas:
    - effort;
    - reporting;
    - timekeeping;
    - honesty;
    - contribution to the sales team's development;
    - anything else you consider important.

2   Ask salespeople to write down what they expect from their relationship with managers in the following areas:
    - honesty;
    - information;
    - trust;
    - communication;
    - opportunities for growth or promotion;
    - other personal requirements.

3   The resulting discussion and agreement on future behaviour should clear the air of any potential negative issues that might otherwise get in the way of an effective working relationship between the parties.

4   These are the terms of engagement and it is important to get these clear from the start.

WORKSHOP   People and Performance Workshop 2:
Creating an Organizational Blueprint

Objective

This workshop is designed to translate sales and customer strategy into an Organizational Blueprint for the rest of the organization.

Process

1   Select a typical customer and identify their usual lifespan, from when they first approach the organization as a prospective customer until they leave due to competitive pressure or for some other reason.

2   Identify, at any stage in this lifespan, any event that could result in a contact of any kind with the organization. These contacts are also called *critical incidents* or moments of truth. They can take many forms, including: initial contact, sales visits, enquiries, information requests, ordering, order status enquiries, billing, customer service requests and complaints.

3   Identify the ideal experience that you would like to provide the customer with at every point of contact, and any specific measurables or outcomes associated with this contact. This experience should reflect the organization's *distinctive competencies* and *competitive positioning*, which are part of the organization's *strategic direction*.

4   Identify the individuals or processes responsible for this experience and ensure their job specification and key deliverables reflect this role. This step often challenges the organization's existing structure and the role of key staff members, which can lead to reorganization, recruitment or training.

5   Ensure that management actions and behaviour support the delivery of this customer experience by paying careful attention to rewards, promotions and any kind of acknowledgement or recognition of performance.

CASE STUDY   People and Performance Case Study 1: Provider of mail delivery services – Creating sales structures and customer portfolios

Background

This international provider of mail collection and delivery services operated a number of different sales and customer service structures in its nine sales divisions around the UK. Typically the company used historical sales revenue as the most important measure of customer importance and allocated accounts accordingly as follows:

- Key account managers (KAMs) – Field-based executives managing customers with the highest historical sales revenues (typically 2–3 accounts).

- Account managers (AMs) – Field-based executives managing the next tier of accounts by historical revenue (typically 20–30 accounts).

- Account executives (AEs) – Office-based executives managing the next tier of accounts by historical revenue using the phone and e-mail (typically 40–80 accounts).

- Telephone account managers (TAMs) – Office-based people managing the smallest accounts by historical revenue using the phone and e-mail (typically 100–150 accounts).

The customer portfolios held by each executive were fixed, which meant that customers or customer opportunities were never passed to another sales executive whatever the circumstances. Each level of sales executive was also given a sales target based on historical sales revenue for each of their accounts.

Typically, all office-based sales executives were located together in groups. Therefore, all AEs sat together in one area of the office and all TAMs sat together in a different area of the office.

The company wanted to better identify customer importance. They also wanted to find the most appropriate sales and customer organizational structure to meet the demands of customers, whether large bulk mailers or smaller organizations where mail was still an important aspect of their business.

Activity

Major external and internal reviews were undertaken. The external review consisted of a research process where a range of customers were interviewed, from the very small to the very large, in order to understand their business requirements and service expectations. The internal review consisted of examining customer portfolios held by the sales team in order to understand how the requirements and expectations of these customers were being met.

Key recommendations

- Key account managers should have national responsibility for the largest and most important accounts, which should not restrict their activity to divisional geography.

- Account managers, account executives and telephone account managers should work together to jointly manage all accounts in a particular geographical area within a division (defined by postcodes). They should collectively be responsible for the growth of that joint and shared customer portfolio in order to provide the most appropriate level of sales attention.

- The AMs, AEs and TAMs should therefore form sales teams and should be given a sales team target.

- The sales teams should be encouraged to pass customers and customer opportunities between themselves to ensure the most appropriate customer response.

- The sales teams should be located together in a particular space within the office to facilitate a team approach to their activities

CASE STUDY   People and Performance Case Study 2:
International truck manufacturer – Creating territory targets

Background

This truck manufacturer allocated sales territories and sales targets based on historical sales information. These territories and targets were felt not to accurately reflect sales potential in the dealer's sales areas, and not to be fair and motivational. The company wanted to move towards a more effective and fairer targeting process.

Activity

In order to identify the sales potential of each dealer territory, a range of information for each geographical territory was collected as follows:

- DVLA registration data showing truck registrations, by individual manufacturer, in each postcode area;

- dealer sales performance and market share by postcode area;

- dealer sales performance showing the extent of dealers' poaching into other dealers' sales areas;

- sales executives' presentations of the structure of their territories and the sales opportunities they felt existed.

This combination of all the above analysis identified the sales potential for each individual dealer, together with the existing effectiveness of the dealer in exploiting this potential.

Key learning points

- Much of the information available for identifying the sales opportunity in each territory was not being used, and as a result business was being lost.

- Salespeople were asked to physically explore their territories in detail and to identify new locations were business might exist.

- The resulting territory targets more accurately reflected sales potential and opportunities.

- The resulting targets were perceived to be fair and motivational, particularly as they were seen to be achievable.

CASE STUDY People and Performance Case Study 3:
Global provider of data transmission infrastructure – Creating
global account teams

Background

This company is a global provider of voice and data transmission infrastructure to mobile telephone operators. The company wanted to put together a number of global account teams to reflect the needs of their largest customers, who typically transcended national market areas.

Activity

A process was developed to identify the requirements of the leading operators of voice and data traffic in each market area. An account team structure was then created that defined the composition of the account teams, together with their individual and joint responsibilities and their reporting relationships to their wider organization. This template contained the following elements:

- overall management control;

- sales and customer responsibilities;

- technical responsibilities;

- allocation of revenue to individuals, to the account team as a whole, and to national sales organizations;

- funding and resource requirements of the team;

- reporting relationships.

Key learning points

- Only those customers that could benefit from global account management were included in the programme. Those customers that were large but generally operated with regional or local autonomy were not included.

- National sales companies were involved in the development of the process and template, and therefore bought into the overall global account team strategy.

CASE STUDY   People and Performance Case Study 4:
Manufacturer of building materials – Identification of key
sales competencies

Background

This company manufactures building materials, especially insulating building blocks that
provide the thermal properties required to meet building regulations. The products are
sold direct to larger builders and contractors and through builders' merchants to smaller
builders. Additionally, architects and specifiers are regularly contacted to secure original
specifications for major building projects.

The company wished to identify those sales attributes most responsible for sales
success (the means). They also wanted to ensure that these were developed across the
entire sales team.

Activity

An initial sales review was conducted to observe salespeople in action and to identify
those sales attributes most responsible for sales success. A number of average sales
performers and top sales performers were chosen in order to isolate those factors most
responsible for sales success.

It became clear that top sales performers brought a number of higher-level competencies to their role, particularly *identifying customer issues and opportunities* and
presenting value propositions. These competencies were themselves a result of higher-
level sales skills such as *questioning*, *probing* and *presenting*. All of the elements
responsible for sales success were then brought together into a competency profile that
defined each of them in detail, as well as the standard of performance expected and how
each of them would be observed and measured.

Key learning points

- The entire sales team was involved at each stage of the process and even signed
  off the resulting competency profile. This profile listed all the key sales attributes,
  together with how they would be used in appraising sales performance. In this way,
  the buy-in and commitment of the sales team to the project was achieved.

- These competencies were then adopted into a field appraisal process that was used
  to improve sales performance across the entire sales team.

- This exercise created the foundations for a continuous process of development
  across the business and was seen to be instrumental in raising performance.

Appendix 1

Example job description: Account manager

The role

Account managers are responsible for all customers in a geographical area. They have a mixture of existing accounts (30–40 each) but are also targeted to win new customers. They are also targeted against customer satisfaction measures provided by customers.

Reporting relationships

Account managers will report to the sales and marketing director. They will also work closely with the telephone account managers.

Key performance measures

Sales targets

- 100 per cent of sales volume target;
- 25 per cent of which must be from new customers;
- stretch target amounting to 120 per cent of sales target also set;
- gross profit margin of 33 per cent required on all sales;
- customer satisfaction required to be 75 per cent.

Intermediate performance measures

- Account plans for the six customers being managed with account plans.
- Activity management measures for the remaining customers.

Competency profile

Competencies

- developing credibility and relationships;
- prospecting and qualifying;
- identifying customer situation and opportunities;
- internal and external networking (a specific competence to the role);
- winning business.

Key sales attributes

Knowledge:

- industry knowledge;
- customer knowledge;
- company knowledge.

Skills:

- listening;
- communicating;
- presenting;
- planning and organizing.

Behaviour:

- energy and enthusiasm;
- initiative;
- professionalism;
- self-motivation.

Standards of performance

Standards of performance should be outlined for each competence, knowledge, skill and behaviour listed above.

An example

Competence: Managing the sales process
Definition: The ability to retain control of the sales process in order to guide the customer towards a successful conclusion.

TABLE 7.14 Managing the sales process performance standard

Performance standard	Performance definition
Above standard	Outstanding ability to manage the sales process and guide the customer towards a successful conclusion
Required standard	Mostly able to manage the sales process and guide the customer towards a successful conclusion
Below standard	Not often able to manage the sales process and guide the customer towards a successful conclusion

Assessment

Key performance measures

- Achievement against sales targets will be assessed on a monthly basis.
- Incentives will be paid quarterly according to performance.
- Customer satisfaction will be assessed quarterly.

Intermediate measures of performance

- Account plans will be discussed monthly and appropriate account strategies agreed.
- Activity management results will be assessed monthly.

Competencies

Account managers will be appraised using the field appraisal document every 4–6 weeks and their personal development plan adjusted accordingly.

Rewards

Details of the appropriate salary and reward scheme.

Appendix 2

Field appraisal document: Account manager

A field appraisal document is a tool the manager uses to monitor sales competencies and their constituent knowledge, skills and behaviours. All the competencies are listed, together with the knowledge, skills and behaviours, and the document contains all the definitions and standards of performance that relate to these.

After observing the salesperson in action over an appropriate period, the manager and salesperson discuss the salesperson's performance and an evaluation is made of whether their performance is *below standard*, *standard* or *above standard*. A discussion will then take place to agree the salesperson's key strengths and weaknesses, and to agree to:

- *Exploit their strengths* – by presenting how they do what they do in a sales meeting, or perhaps by mentoring another member of the sales team.
- *Address their weaknesses* – through training, coaching or mentoring from another individual in the sales team.

Example competence element: *Managing the sales process*

TABLE 7.15   Managing the sales process performance standard

Standard of performance	Performance definition
Above standard	Outstanding ability to manage the sales process and guide the customer towards a successful conclusion
Required standard	Mostly able to manage the sales process and guide the customer towards a successful conclusion
Below standard	Not often able to manage the sales process and guide the customer towards a successful conclusion

Agreed evaluation

Agreed actions

Date of next review

08

Development and motivation

How can we help people give of their best?

FIGURE 8.1 The Business Performance Value Chain: Development and Motivation

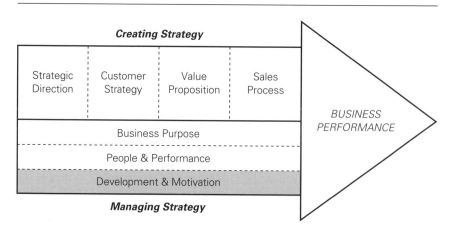

In this final chapter of Part Three we will first look at development, which is about helping people to fulfil their potential using appraisal, training and coaching. We will then look at motivation, which looks to identify what is important to individuals and how these aspirations can be harnessed for the benefit of the organization, as well as for the benefit of the individual concerned.

Development

Development is helping people to become better at those things that will make them more successful in their role in support of organizational objectives. When we looked at *performance* in the previous chapter, we discussed *ends* and *means*. In this section we are going to look at how to develop the *means*; that is, how to develop the necessary elements that lead to performance.

In order to be effective, a development strategy needs the following:

1 A detailed description of the competences required to perform the specific role in question, together with their constituent knowledge, skills and behaviours.

2 A means to measure and assess these elements.

3 A means to develop these skills in others and to generally raise the standard of performance across all salespeople.

Therefore, in addition to raising performance, a well-grounded development strategy is also highly motivational. It provides opportunities for achievement, feedback, recognition, advancement and growth – all key determinants of satisfaction and motivation, which we will discuss in the next section.

When we looked at *performance* earlier, we looked at the first two of these aspects and created a *competency profile* for an account manager and an *appraisal process*. The field appraisal process will therefore provide the opportunity to identify the development requirements of individuals and of the entire sales organization, creating a personal development plan for the individual and a training needs analysis (TNA) for the whole sales organization.

The personal development plan

A personal development plan records the following:

- the results of the field appraisal;
- agreements between the manager and salesperson as to the appropriate courses of action, eg coaching;
- a record of those actions.

Each salesperson should ideally have a personal development plan, which records their performance as measured by their competencies, attributes and standards of performance. This document also records the agreement between the salesperson and management as to how certain levels of performance are to be developed.

Training needs analysis

A training needs analysis (TNA) is usually conducted for a whole sales organization to assess its level of performance against specified performance criteria as a prelude to creating a development and training plan. The existence of defined competencies, attributes and standards of performance, as utilized by the sales appraisal form and personal development plan, provide the best possible means of creating a TNA.

Creating a philosophy of development

The creation of a development philosophy across the sales organization has three main objectives:

- to help individuals and groups achieve their potential;
- to motivate individuals and groups to strive for higher levels of performance;
- to improve the performance of the organization in the pursuit of its vision and goals.

A positive philosophy of development recognizes when people are doing the right things and encourages them to continue to strive towards their personal and organizational goals. Furthermore, it seeks to spread this positive climate of personal achievement across the entire organization by helping the less effective performers to approach the level of the best performers.

This runs counter to the opposite philosophy that only seems to recognize the best performers without attempting to help others achieve similar performance levels. This opposite philosophy only seems to identify when people are doing 'wrong' rather than when they are doing 'right'.

Furthermore, the development philosophy makes another important assumption. It recognizes that although some people seem to be born with different abilities or more natural gifts: *everybody can develop higher levels of performance, given the right encouragement and support.*

This is not to say that everyone has the ability to become a star performer, but it does mean that every person has the ability to improve their capabilities and levels of performance. This will benefit both the individual and the organization as a whole. It means that although good salespeople can be born, everyone can be made better!

Training v coaching

Both training and coaching are important elements of development, but they work in slightly different ways. Training is quite formal in nature, as it usually seeks to transfer the right way of doing something to an individual. Training would therefore be appropriate in helping someone to learn CPR or how to make interesting presentations.

Coaching, on the other hand, is normally less formal and less narrowly defined. Rather than being concerned with helping someone to learn a specific skill, coaching is more about encouraging individuals to think or act differently in situations they may find themselves in.

Coaching is more likely to be effective if the basic skills relating to an activity are already present. For example, it would be very difficult to coach someone to win customer business if they did not already possess the basic sales skills of questioning, presenting and closing.

Coaching is therefore more appropriate in developing competencies and higher-level skills and behaviours, whereas training is normally more appropriate for developing knowledge and more basic skills. These are not hard and fast rules, however, as a combination of both is usually required as part of an overall development process. Mentoring is similar to coaching, as it looks to encourage individuals to develop different and more effective behaviours.

Developing competencies

We spent a lot of time in the previous chapter in defining the levels of performance that are expected. This is an essential step in the development process, as clear benchmarks are needed to show people what they should be able to do. The organization must now ensure that it has the means to bring its people up to these levels of performance through development.

Returning to the *sales performance framework*, the focus will be on developing those sales competencies that provide the means to achieve sales performance. The list of generic competencies that were considered were:

- prospecting and qualifying;
- developing credibility and relationships;
- identifying customer situation and opportunities;
- presenting value propositions;
- obtaining customer commitment;
- managing the sales process;
- territory and time management.

Note: Every sales role may require different sales competencies and these can only be identified through observation and analysis. These are typical capabilities that are demonstrated more often by the better sales performers and are therefore abilities that are positively linked to sales success.

Once competencies have been correctly defined, they are relatively easy to observe. It is easy to identify a good golfer by how well they drive off the tee, hit fairway shots, chip onto the green and then roll the ball into the hole. In the same way, it is relatively easy to identify a good salesperson by how they develop credibility and relationships, identify the customer situation and opportunities, present value propositions and then finally obtain customer commitment. The key question is therefore: if the above sales competencies are closely linked with sales performance, how should they be developed?

Given what we have previously said about training and coaching, it is probably the latter method that is more appropriate for developing competencies, assuming that salespeople already possess the necessary knowledge, skills and behaviours. The coaching of competencies is therefore best achieved by explaining how particular elements of knowledge, skills and behaviours are brought together in a specific way to produce the right result.

Demonstration is also an important part of coaching, where the right way to do something is shown and the individual is then encouraged to try the behaviour themselves. Role play is then an important way for an individual to practise these new behaviours.

Developing knowledge, skills and behaviours

A process is needed that develops these sales attributes across the entire sales team, where:

- knowledge is *acquired*;
- skills are *practised*;
- behaviours are *learned* or *changed*.

Acquiring knowledge

It is normally felt that *knowledge* is probably the easiest of the three attributes to develop. The basic knowledge that a salesperson needs to have in order to be effective includes knowledge of the:

- market environment;
- customer business issues;
- company proposition/competitive positioning;
- company procedures.

Such things can be learned without too much difficulty from a mixture of various sources: internal documentation, existing staff, management action or via a formal staff induction programme. To use a golf or a hockey example, the rules that apply to these sports can be acquired from reading a book on the subject from the relevant sporting association.

Practising skills

After knowledge, *skills* are thought to occupy the next level of difficulty, in that they are harder to develop than knowledge but easier to develop than behaviours. Unlike knowledge, which is acquired, skills are developed through practice, and the person must first become familiar with the principles upon which this practice should be based.

The generic list of the most important skills for salespeople includes:

- listening;
- questioning and probing;
- communicating and presenting;
- trading value and negotiating;
- closing;
- analysing and planning.

To continue with the sporting examples, in golf the skill of putting can only be learned through repeated practice on the greens once the fundamentals of grip and swing are known. Similarly in hockey, the skill of dribbling can only be developed through repeated practice on the hockey pitch.

However, a mere list of the necessary skills is not enough. As discussed in the last chapter on performance and illustrated in the competency profile we developed for an account manager, these skills must be described as accurately as possible, but there is also a need to define *performance standards* for how these skills should be measured.

Learning and changing behaviours

In this book the term *behaviour* has been used rather than the term *attitude*. This reflects the point that certain internal attitudes do not necessarily have to result in certain behaviours. It is the behaviour rather than the attitude that we are interested in observing and developing.

This is particularly important as there has always been a debate as to whether attitudes can actually be changed or developed. By focusing on behaviour rather than on attitude, it is more likely that a change in performance can be encouraged.

Let us look at *desire*, which is an important attitude in sales. Can you just say to a salesperson, 'Hey, you, I want you to show increased desire'?

This is a doubtful strategy for a number of reasons. First, what is meant by desire and how does the person know whether they have it? Secondly, is it something they can actually change?

We therefore need to define what is meant by desire, by breaking it down into constituent parts that can be understood, observed or measured. *Desire* may thus be defined as:

- the amount of effort expended;
- the levels of sales activity;
- the willingness to take on a challenge.

The above definitions are now more concrete and less vague, and all of them are observable and measurable. Because of this, this behaviour can now be discussed in a more meaningful way. Furthermore, it can also now be pointed out whether this behaviour is lacking in any way, which is the first step towards behaviour change.

Coaching

Coaching is one of the most important ways that sales managers add value to their sales organization. It is particularly appropriate in developing competencies, more advanced sales skills, and behaviours.

Coaching should also be developmental, in that it should be focused on improving performance. The best coaching is where the salesperson is helped to understand their own strengths and weaknesses and is therefore more engaged and committed to any improvement actions.

There are two types of coaching in sales:

- Skills coaching: Where managers look to develop the necessary sales competencies.
- Strategy coaching: Where managers help to develop account strategy.

Skills coaching

Figure 8.2 identifies the opportunities for skills coaching. Basically, these opportunities exist at every point of the sales process, as outlined below.

As previously discussed, *standards of performance* can be created for all those skills necessary at each stage of the sales process. Salespeople can then be observed in action to monitor and measure these standards using the field appraisal process. This provides a measure of performance for each salesperson at every point of the sales process, which supplies the information managers require to identify the need for coaching.

A skills coaching model

The following provides a practical framework for skills coaching:

1 Focus on the good points.
2 Get salespeople to identify their own strengths and weaknesses.

FIGURE 8.2   Opportunities for skills coaching

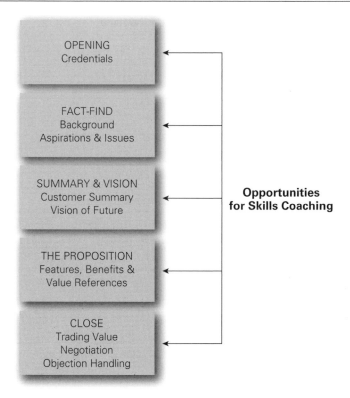

3 Discuss the issues – causes and implications.

4 Pick one issue to deal with.

5 Agree coaching or training input.

6 Follow up.

Strategy coaching

Strategy coaching is where managers look to help develop account strategy for the most important customers by stimulating the right thinking and actions. In the same way that crucial moments of truth exist in the customer journey, there are key points in the account strategy that reflect what is going on within the customer. These are key coaching opportunities for the sales manager to add value to the whole strategic process. When selecting those accounts to strategy coach and choosing the frequency and timing of these reviews, these key coaching opportunities should be borne in mind.

The catalyst for strategy coaching is the account plan, as shown in Figure 8.3. Strategy coaching should revolve around the three areas identified in this diagram: overall goal, objectives and strategy, and resources.

FIGURE 8.3   Opportunities for strategy coaching

Overall goal

This is the most important aspect of the strategy, which relates to the end point of the process. Such a goal can be stated in a number of ways and is of course specific to the account in question and the current position within that account.

The goal might be stated in traditional ways such as customer share or sales volume. However, a realistic goal could be to establish a foothold in the account, to establish a presence in some way, and so on.

Objectives and strategy

This refers to how the overall goal is to be met. For example, an initial objective might be to identify the decision-making unit (DMU) or the decision-making process (DMP).

Having done this, the next objective could be to identify a coach, to help us find our way around the customer. In this way, individual objectives are the stepping stones to the overall goal and link together as an account strategy.

Resources

An account strategy takes time and resources. Such things should also be a part of any strategy coaching process.

Starting strategy coaching

Because of time constraints, it is probably impossible to review all account plans for every account manager. The best ones to pick for the review process are those that are nearer the start of the whole process, ie where the account manager has just started the research and the entry strategy.

Additionally, those customers that will give the best opportunities for discussion of strategy and tactics should be chosen for review. The continual review of these accounts will thus create a learning and development experience that will hopefully influence the account management of the remaining customers.

Ideally, then, the process should start with a few key accounts and key development accounts for each account manager, as these will provide the best opportunities for strategy coaching. In order to ensure that account planning is effective, sales management should:

- carry out account reviews regularly, say once every two weeks;
- review the same accounts to provide continuity and effective follow-up;
- examine progress since the last review and agree those actions that will take the account strategy and plan to the next step;
- agree the timing and expectations of the next review.

Team development

So far we have been concentrating on individual development. It is now time to focus on groups of people or teams. But given that B2B sales is often a solitary profession, why should we be concerned with teams?

A specific example of the importance of teams is clearly the account team, where a number of individuals with particular skills come together to service a specific account. This situation was dealt with in earlier chapters. But apart from account teams, a team approach in sales is advantageous under a number of headings.

Improved effectiveness

The opportunity to share experiences and best practice around the team contributes to overall sales effectiveness and sales performance.

Developmental advantages

The chance to raise overall performance by identifying the sales competencies most associated with sales success provides an opportunity to raise the performance of all members of the team. Additionally, the ability to allocate specific roles or projects to individual team members on behalf of the team is helpful in both development and motivation. Furthermore, the competitive element provided by the group can also be motivational, provided that such competition is kept positive and productive.

Social advantages

The importance of social interaction and mutual support should not be under-estimated. Opportunities provided by sales meetings or other get-togethers provide a valuable means to meet the need for social interaction.

Team life cycles

Just as with most sports, the throwing together of a group of individuals does not automatically produce a team. All groups and teams have a life cycle that is shown in Figure 8.4.

FIGURE 8.4   Sales team development: Stages in the team life cycle

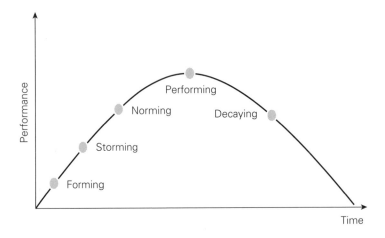

Forming

During this first stage of the life cycle, when individuals find themselves members of a new team, the expectations, objectives, roles and responsibilities are unclear. Team members spend a lot of time during this stage simply getting to know each other. This degree of uncertainty produces considerable anxiety for all members of the team, as they are unsure of their own position and role within the team.

Storming

During this next stage of the team life cycle, team members come to better understand the nature of the overall team tasks, objectives and expectations. They also begin to clarify the roles and responsibilities within the team.

Team members are starting to produce ideas about how the team should work and about how team tasks should be addressed. There may, however, be a degree of conflict and of jostling for position evident within the team.

Norming

During this stage in the team's development, roles and responsibilities become clear and the real work of the team begins. The team starts to allocate specific roles based on specific skills and expertise, and demonstrates a more participative style of team-working.

Performing

This stage represents the ultimate goal of team development, as the team's output and performance reaches its peak. Team roles and responsibilities are now relatively fixed, with everyone within the team knowing how they fit in and what is expected of them. As a result, a high degree of participation and collaboration is evident across the team.

Decaying

Even the best teams lose their effectiveness over time. This is either because the need for the team disappears or because the team starts to lose its effectiveness. Effectiveness can be lost for a variety of reasons but normally because the team has failed to develop and evolve.

In the same way that team cohesion first led to the team's effectiveness, this closeness and insularity eventually leads to the team's reduction in effectiveness and subsequent demise. A resistance to new ideas that originate from outside of the team and a resistance to potential new members are the main reasons for the team's eventual insularity.

Implications for management

Given the above typical team life cycle, what can management do to speed up the development of the team and to retain the team's effectiveness over time? Figure 8.5 outlines the appropriate management interventions at each stage of the team life cycle.

Management intervention: Forming

The objective of management action during this stage in development is to provide as much clarity as possible. In particular, clarity should be provided about the role of the team, its objectives and expectations. This should begin to reduce the uncertainty and anxiety that affects the team during this stage, which will pave the way for the acclimatization of each team member.

FIGURE 8.5   Management interventions in the team life cycle

FORMING
Confusion / Uncertainty
Getting acquainted

Be clear about objectives & expectations

Provide some guidance about team roles & responsibilities

STORMING
Disagreements
Tensions Hostility

Make time for important issues & be clear about direction & purpose

Address any specific conflicts

NORMING
Consensus / Leaders
Stable roles

Support the team making its own decisions

Support the team allocating specific team roles & responsibilities

PERFORMING
Success / Openness

Delegate & stretch people

Encourage innovation or introduce new tasks

DECAYING
Decreasing effectiveness
Concern more for
team than tasks

Add new blood or add new ideas to the team

Consider reforming or disbanding team

Additionally, management should give team members the opportunity to get to know each other by providing time for social interaction.

This approach to management action during this stage of the team life cycle is in line with the notion of *situational leadership*, which suggests that management action should be appropriate and proportionate to the situation faced. In the *forming* stage, situational leadership implies that management input should be *directive*.

Management intervention: Storming

The objective of management action during this stage of team development is to further encourage socialization within the team and the development of individual team roles. Management may be called upon to address specific areas of conflict that the team has not yet been able to resolve, but the overall nature of management at this point is one of gradual withdrawal from the initial directive stance into a style that is more consultative. In the *storming* stage, the situational leadership approach supports this notion of a move towards a more *coaching* or *selling* style of management.

Management intervention: Norming

During this stage, management should encourage the continued development of the team ethic and the allocation of individual responsibilities. Management should therefore move even further away from its initial directive stance towards a more *supportive* role. This is again in line with the situational leadership model of management action.

Management intervention: Performing

This is the stage of maximum team performance and therefore the team's assets should be sweated, which means that all available performance should be extracted from the team. Management should look to stretch the team further by either increasing the complexity of its tasks or by adding further responsibilities to the team.

At this stage the team is effectively self-supportive and is running itself, and therefore it requires little management intervention. During the *performing* stage, situational leadership implies that management input should be based on *delegation*.

Management intervention: Decaying

If team performance should reduce, management can consider a number of actions. It may attempt to breathe new life into the team by introducing new members or new ideas, or it can re-form the team or give it entirely new tasks and objectives. Should this fail to work, another option is to disband the team entirely.

Note on recruitment

How should this discussion on performance affect the recruitment process? Given that it is easier to acquire knowledge and to develop skills than to change behaviours, then perhaps the recruitment and selection process should put increased emphasis on identifying those behaviours that are seen to be most closely linked to sales performance.

This runs counter to the traditional practice in recruitment, which often over-emphasizes existing knowledge (gained through experience) compared to the ability to gain new skills and to change behaviour. Recruitment should also recognize that achievement orientation is an important requisite for sales performance (see the section below on motivation).

Motivation

The subject of *motivation* is by far the most important topic that comes up when you ask sales managers about their biggest concerns. Motivation has almost achieved the status of a 'black art' in some circles; it is often talked about but perhaps much less understood.

So just what is motivation? Perhaps a definition will be useful: *Motivation is a process that explains how people can be encouraged to adopt specific behaviours in pursuit of specific objectives.*

In a sales situation, motivation is the way that people are encouraged to improve their performance or to strive harder towards a specific objective or target. It can be either positive or negative in its effect. Motivation is positive when encouraging a movement towards something desirable, or negative when encouraging a movement away from something undesirable.

There is a view that positive motivation is ultimately more powerful than the negative kind. Pushing someone into the water will certainly get them swimming in order to avoid drowning (assuming they can swim), but it will hardly create an enduring passion for the water. Similarly, threatening people with negative consequences such as dismissal or the hair-dryer treatment might work in the short term, but it is unlikely to generate a positive climate of improved performance in the long run.

In this section we will therefore consider some of the different theories of motivation and work towards the development of a practical framework that can be used to allow people to give of their best. Let's first look at motivation by considering the following exercise, which demonstrates some important principles.

A motivation exercise

When I drive my car normally without checking on fuel consumption, I achieve about 32 mpg. But when I focus on fuel consumption on a real-time basis using the car's trip computer, I can fairly easily achieve 37 mpg and can even achieve 40 mpg if I pull out all the stops. This equates to a minimum of a 15 per cent improvement, with 25 per cent at a stretch.

What's going on here?

- First, the *result*, fuel economy, is important to me and significant enough for me to strive for it.
- The notion of improving fuel economy by 5 mph through altering my driving style was *a valuable and achievable challenge*.

- The *stretch target* of achieving 40 mpg was more difficult, requiring even greater levels of focus and skill.

- Finally, I was getting *instant and positive feedback* on the result, which *encouraged me to continue* to see how much further I could push it.

What this exercise seems to demonstrate is that in order to motivate, a number of requirements need to be satisfied:

- The objective has to be desirable and achievable.

- The ability to perform at the necessary level to achieve the objective should exist.

- The early provision of performance-related feedback should reinforce and encourage the right level of effort.

So has this provided a framework for developing motivation? Well, before we get too carried away, let's make sure the framework is in agreement with the more traditional theories of motivation and see whether anything further can be learned.

Some traditional theories of motivation

The following diagram identifies some of the most important theories of motivation, which will be explored further below.

FIGURE 8.6   Motivation theories

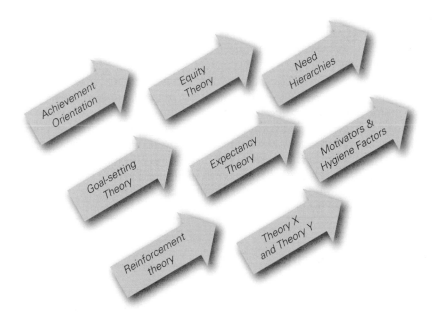

Achievement orientation

Achievement orientation relates to how much individuals feel compelled to achieve things. In everyday experience it does seem that some people are more inclined to accept challenges and to strive towards goals than others. An individual's achievement motivation could therefore be said to be a measure of their inner drive. Drive has always been a popular word found in most recruitment adverts for commercial jobs, as it is seen as an essential quality in the business world.

The notion of achievement orientation also states that the end result should be desirable in order to strongly influence behaviour towards the achievement of that result. It stands to reason, therefore, that achievement orientation is felt to be a desirable trait in most salespeople.

Furthermore, the research suggests that those people with a need for achievement have the following characteristics:

- They enjoy tasks of moderate difficulty – not too easy, but not so difficult as to be viewed as impossible.

- They set realistic goals – they won't aim to double sales, but might expect to increase them by 20–30 per cent.

- They seek out and use feedback on their performance – they particularly welcome constructive criticism and will act on it.

- They take personal responsibility for their performance – accepting praise for high performance and accepting responsibility for poor performance.

This theory of achievement motivation raises an important practical point for the recruitment of individuals who will be expected to achieve specific results and performance targets. It suggests that organizations should attempt to measure the achievement motivation of those individuals being considered for such highly visible, performance-oriented roles.

We have already discussed the competencies associated with successful salespeople and have identified both *desire* and *self-motivation* as being behaviours linked to high performance. As both of these competencies are related to achievement motivation, by looking for particular signs of desire and motivation during any recruitment and selection process, the organization can test for the existence of achievement motivation in the candidates.

As far as the motivational framework mentioned earlier is concerned, it would appear that it does reflect the importance of achievement motivation. It includes the need for desirable results, realistic goals, personal responsibility and performance feedback.

Goal-setting theory

For people in business, *goal-setting theory* is probably one of the easiest theories to accept, as it is based on the notion that targets stimulate performance.

This theory suggests that the intention to work towards a specific goal is a major source of motivation and that more difficult goals, if accepted, result in higher performance than easier goals.

The theory goes further by suggesting that the existence of performance feedback, particularly self-generated feedback, leads to higher performance than if there was no feedback at all. There is also a suggestion that participation in setting harder goals increases the likelihood of these goals being accepted.

An individual's motivation towards the achievement of commercial goals would seem to be a prerequisite of success in the commercial environment. Any selection and recruitment process looking to identify individuals for key commercial roles should therefore evaluate how they have responded to goals in the past, in order to establish whether they have had a positive influence on behaviour.

In the competency framework discussed in the previous chapter, *tenacity*, *self-motivation*, *diligence* and *desire* were included as behaviours linked to sales performance. Since all of these behaviours seem to be associated with the achievement of goals, their identification in any individual would bode well for the achievement of goals being a positive motivator for that person.

The motivation framework would seem to reflect this theory very well. It be must remembered that the ultimate goal should be specific and that sufficient stretch should be provided to promote maximum performance, whilst simultaneously ensuring that the goal remains achievable.

Reinforcement theory

Reinforcement theory is a very simple theory that originated from behavioural psychology. It suggests that rewards will encourage positive behaviours, while punishments will discourage negative behaviours.

The theory is more interested in the behaviour exhibited than in what is going on in the mind of the individual concerned. It's the old notion of the carrot and the stick – if you do something good you receive a reward; if you do something bad you receive a punishment.

Transferring this theory to the commercial environment suggests that management has a key role in reinforcing certain activities and behaviours. As we saw in Chapter 6 on culture, managers and leaders can strongly encourage (and therefore reinforce) certain behaviours by what they give their attention to and what they reward. Management can thus reinforce desired levels of performance by rewarding the achievement of commercial targets and objectives. They can also reinforce the need to develop the key sales competencies and key sales attributes by setting up a performance framework that monitors and measures all of these elements.

Management can therefore encourage (and reinforce) those sales competencies and sales attributes that are closely associated with sales performance. Simply by monitoring and measuring such things as prospecting and qualifying, presenting value propositions, obtaining customer commitment, knowledge of the market environment, listening, questioning and probing, professionalism, initiative and diligence, management can reinforce their importance and development.

Our framework does appear to reflect reinforcement theory by making it clear that positive and appropriate behaviour should be encouraged, rather than behaviour that is potentially destructive and at variance with team or organizational well-being. This is particularly important when individual objectives and targets may encourage selfish actions that conflict with team or organizational goals.

Equity theory

Equity theory is based on the notion of fairness. It suggests that people have a strong sense of what is fair and what is not, and that this perception will influence how they perceive certain situations and how they respond to them.

This sense of fairness is also a relative measure, as individuals compare themselves with others in similar situations before coming to a particular view of what is fair. For example, they may become demotivated if they perceive unfairness between what they put into something and what they get out of it, particularly if they think that others are getting a better deal.

As discussed previously in terms of culture, management actions are closely scrutinized and set the tone for the whole organization. Fairness is a key aspect under scrutiny and managers must ensure that they are seen to be fair in order to avoid discontent. This is very important in the commercial environment, where targets, incentives and rewards are commonplace and thus provide endless opportunities for managers to fall foul of this essential perception of fairness and equity.

This helps to explain why so many target and incentive schemes seem to do more harm than good. For example, geographically based sales targets are sometimes seen as unfair, as they often reflect historical sales patterns rather than true market potential.

Anything perceived as biased, loaded or generally unfair will turn people off rather than turn them on. The motivational framework must therefore ensure that fairness (to all) is transparent.

Expectancy theory

Expectancy theory states that people are motivated when they can see a clear link between what they put in and what they get out, particularly if what they get out is what they want. Individuals will therefore expend effort in doing something if they anticipate that the end result is in line with what they *expect*. As an example, if a salesperson achieves a bonus of £10 with every unit sold, the salesperson will *expect* £100 if 10 units are sold.

Managers must therefore ensure that there is a clear link between effort and reward; in particular, that more effort will result in a proportionately higher reward. If this relationship does not hold, then individuals can become demotivated. Our framework seems to recognize this by incorporating clear feedback about the results of effort.

Theory X and Theory Y

Theory X and Theory Y is a famous motivation theory developed by the psychologist Douglas McGregor. He suggested two basic but contrasting assumptions about human behaviour – *Theory X* was largely negative in how it viewed human behaviour, and *Theory Y* was largely positive in how it viewed human behaviour.

Theory X suggested that people:

- disliked work and would seek to avoid it;
- would therefore have to be coerced and forced to work;
- would shy away from responsibility and need to be told what to do;
- placed security above everything and had little ambition.

Theory Y, on the other hand, suggested that people:

- view work as being as natural as rest or play;
- will exercise self-direction and control if they support objectives;
- will accept or even seek out responsibility;
- will make creative decisions about their jobs and not simply rely on management.

The two theories are therefore based on two totally opposite views of human behaviour, and will have very different implications for how people should be managed and motivated.

Managers who favour Theory X believe that the only way they can get individuals to perform is to coerce them in some way. These managers will be largely distrustful and suspicious of their subordinates' behaviour and are likely to monitor them very closely. Such managers may operate a micro-management style and be very rule-driven. They are likely to rely on the carrot and stick approach to management, with an absence of trust.

Theory Y, on the other hand, might be described as a more grown-up style of management, where individuals are given responsibility and are expected to perform in line with their potential. The management style is likely to be more relaxed but supportive, creating an environment where individuals can perform.

It is thought that both approaches can be effective, depending on the specific situation, the organizational maturity of the individuals involved, and the nature of the task. So does our framework reflect this theory? It probably does, but it is very much at the Theory Y end of the spectrum.

Need hierarchy

The psychologist Abraham Maslow hypothesized that people have a hierarchy of five needs that they seek to satisfy in a specific order of priority. They start with the first need, satisfy that and then move on to the next. They will continue to move upwards until all of the needs have been met.

The theory suggests that each level of need will only motivate as long as it remains unfulfilled, but as each level of need is met, it ceases to be a motivator. The next level in the hierarchy then takes over as the primary motivator. In this way, as each need is satisfied, the next level of need becomes dominant.

Level 1: Physiological needs

These relate to the basic physical needs like warmth, food and shelter. Once level 1 needs are met, individuals will strive to satisfy their level 2 needs.

Level 2: Safety needs

These relate to the need to protect oneself from physical and emotional harm. Once these needs are met, individuals will strive to satisfy level 3 needs.

Level 3: Social needs

These relate to the need for affection, belongingness and friendship. Once these needs are met, individuals will strive to satisfy their level 4 needs.

Level 4: Esteem needs

These relate to the need for self-respect, status, attention and respect from others. Once these needs are met, individuals will strive to satisfy level 5 needs.

Level 5: Self-actualization

This level is the pinnacle of existence. Individuals at this stage have become what they are capable of becoming. They have reached a state of self-fulfilment.

The main points to take from the theory of need hierarchy are that people's needs can become so satisfied that they are no longer motivated by the same things. For example, if you have £5m in the bank, the theory suggests that earning another £50,000 may not be that important to you.

This theory also suggests that some motivators may lose their power over time and become boring and commonplace. Playing my fuel consumption game is fun and distracting for a while, but it eventually gets boring. I might therefore need some other ways of motivating me to save fuel.

Also, people may be stimulated to move up the hierarchy to fulfil higher-level needs, but as soon as more basic needs are threatened, they will move back down again. If lower-level needs are endangered, they once again become motivators and must be secured. An example of this might be an individual who complains that his or her job does not interest or fulfil them any longer; this dissatisfaction is quickly forgotten if the possibility of redundancy threatens their ability to pay the mortgage.

Our framework does not inherently reflect this hierarchy, so we need to be aware of its notions of levels of needs and their relative power.

Motivation–hygiene theory

In a famous research study, the psychologist Frederick Herzberg asked people what they most liked and disliked about their jobs. Those things that they liked and that gave them satisfaction, he called *motivators*:

- achievement;
- recognition;
- the work itself;
- responsibility;
- advancement;
- growth.

Those things that they did not like and that made them feel dissatisfied with their jobs, he called *hygiene factors*:

- company policy and administration;
- supervision and the relationship with the supervisor;
- working conditions;
- salary;
- relationships with others.

He found that the opposite of *dissatisfaction* was not *satisfaction*. Relieving an aspect of the job that was causing dissatisfaction, such as working conditions, removed its negative impact but did not in itself create a positive climate of motivation. This is similar to saying that having no money creates unhappiness, while having money removes this unhappiness without necessarily creating happiness.

Herzberg also suggested that in order to motivate, you must first remove those hygiene factors that lead to demotivation (such as problems with company rules and regulations). You can then focus on the things that actually motivate, such as recognizing achievement. Our own framework must therefore focus on those factors that are truly motivational, whilst recognizing that demotivators must be removed before the motivators can be effective.

Implications for the initial framework

So what has been learned from this brief tour of traditional motivational theory? We can conclude that our initial framework is pretty sound, as long as it:

- appreciates that different people are motivated by different things;
- accepts that there are hierarchies of need;
- removes demotivators before focusing on the things that motivate;
- sets tough, stretching yet achievable goals;
- rewards appropriate behaviour but ensures that the achievement of individual goals does not conflict with team or organizational goals;
- provides for positive, self-generated feedback;
- provides for early success and rewards.

With these points in mind, let's develop the motivational framework into something a little more sophisticated.

The motivational framework

FIGURE 8.7   The sales motivation framework

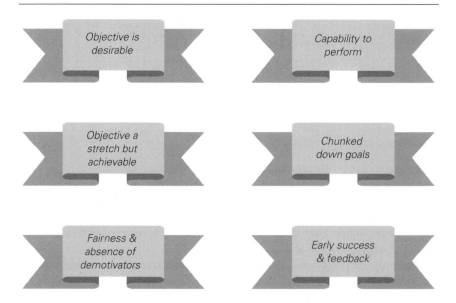

The framework shown in Figure 8.7 indicates that any management effort to generate motivation must ensure:

The end result is desirable: I want this

Knowledge of what is important to people and where they are currently positioned in their hierarchy of needs allows the organization to enter into a *psychological contract* with each individual.

A psychological contract is an understanding that exists between two parties where each party is prepared to do something for the other, provided they get back what they want in return. Employees and employers can therefore have a psychological contract. Parties in a marriage can also have a psychological contract. Likewise, friends can have a psychological contract.

Some individuals, for example, may tolerate routine and repetitive jobs if they provide them with opportunities for social interaction. Other people, such as teachers and nurses, may be satisfied with a fairly low-paying job if it fulfils their need to care for others, give something back to the community, or make a difference. Still others may only take jobs that give them a sense of personal power or status, which is more important to them than anything else.

Of course, there are many factors that influence what jobs people do, but we have to accept that people are different and do not all respond to the same sense of what is important and valuable. There are people who spend most of their lives in freezing conditions looking after wolves, and others who devote their lives to caring for the sick and dying in remote African states.

In a sales situation, individual salespeople will strive for targets if they personally perceive the rewards to be worthwhile. Some members of a sales team may also be prepared to do things that they do not personally see as important if it contributes towards team success. You must therefore open your mind in order to understand what motivates others, and accept that such things may be very different from what motivates you.

So how can you find out what motivates particular individuals? There are a number of ways, indirect and direct, as outlined below.

Ask them what they like most about this job or any previous job

This is an example of an indirect approach. It is useful in bringing out revealing aspects of an individual's personality and particular motivators.

The person may talk about having responsibility, exercising authority, learning new things, achieving difficult goals, working as part of a team, developing new business ideas, closing sales, or earning lots of money. The list is potentially endless, but the passion and enthusiasm that people demonstrate when they talk about the things that are really important to them is very obvious and is a good indicator of what motivates them.

Ask them what they do or enjoy outside of work

This is another indirect approach and addresses the fact that individuals can achieve satisfaction from many different aspects of life. How people satisfy their needs outside of work can therefore be very revealing.

For example, individuals may fulfil their need for status, social interaction and belonging to a community by becoming a school governor, magistrate, community policeman or member of a local charity organization. As these people are satisfying these needs outside the work environment, they may not be motivated by the same things within work and may need different things within the work environment. Alternatively, it may be that some individuals have pursued satisfaction outside the work situation because it was not forthcoming within it.

Perhaps the main implication from this discussion is that in order to find out what motivates any individual, the whole person must be understood. It should also be remembered that people's situations can change, and therefore their needs and motivations can change as well.

Ask them directly what they want from a work situation

This is the direct approach and may work better with some people. They will typically raise the sorts of things listed in the section on Herzberg's motivation–hygiene theory above, such as recognition and achievement in the plus section, and working conditions and company policy on the negative side.

All of the above conversations are best carried out outside of the office in a less formal environment, in order to bring about a more open exchange and discussion. As more examples are revealed of what individuals do and do not find rewarding, a *motivational profile* for each person can constructed. This will help to ensure that you press the right buttons to motivate each individual and provide them with the satisfaction they are looking for, whilst simultaneously producing the levels of performance the business is looking for – a win-win.

Why not try out this approach by testing your own motivation through asking yourself these questions? You might be interested in the answers...

The objective is a stretch but achievable: This is possible

The fuel consumption example at the beginning of this section demonstrated this point, with up to 40 mpg being achievable at a stretch. This suggests that for targets to be motivational they need to be stretching, yet achievable.

This is in line with *goal-setting theory*, which argues that the mere existence of goals is motivational, provided of course that there is an appropriate level of *achievement orientation* within the individual to drive them towards the achievement of these goals. Motivation can be made even stronger if personal goals and organizational goals can be achieved at the same time.

There is fairness and absence of demotivators: This is fair

It has already been shown that fairness and equity are key aspects of motivation and the link between effort and right reward must be clearly demonstrated. The removal of demotivators must also be a priority, otherwise valuable energy and effort will be wasted on hassling over things that are not ultimately important to performance.

There is capability to perform: I know what to do

In the fuel economy example, it was very clear what had to be done to get the results. By accelerating less vigorously, maintaining a constant speed, not going too fast, and anticipating the need to brake in advance, it was possible to have a significant impact on fuel economy. In a sales environment, management must ensure that salespeople have the necessary means to achieve their objectives, not only in terms of the right knowledge, skills and attitudes, but also by providing the necessary supportive environment and culture to foster success.

Chunked-down goals: I can get success quickly

Objectives that are set too far in the future are not sufficiently motivational because efforts made to achieve them do not produce results for some considerable time. There needs to be a faster link between effort expended and results obtained. Ideally this link should be instantaneous, as it was with the fuel consumption example. Fuel economy was instantaneously displayed in fractions of a gallon and this broke the overall objective down into smaller chunks, as the figures changed quickly from 37.0 to 37.1 to 37.2 and so on, all the way to the overall objective. This produced a feeling of achievement and success and generated a desire to do better still.

That's why annual targets should be broken into monthly objectives, and smaller but achievable goals set whenever possible. This is done to bring objectives closer, but also because it provides a means of generating a momentum of success (see below).

Early success and feedback: I'm succeeding

In the car example, if I were only given the results of my fuel economy exercise at the end of the year, it would not be at all interesting or motivational. There must therefore be a rigorous process for measuring, evaluating and communicating performance and for feeding these results back quickly to individuals or groups.

As a general rule, the earlier and more constructive the feedback on performance is, the better its impact will be. This feedback should be on both of the aspects of performance discussed earlier – the *ends* and *means* – that is, how well the individual is doing on meeting objectives, but also how they are measuring up to those actions and behaviours that generate this achievement.

Nothing succeeds like success. The car example, with its progressively achievable wins in fuel economy, generated the momentum of success necessary to move towards the ultimate objective of 40 mpg. Cognitive behavioural therapy supports this theory by suggesting that actual personal experience of successful performance increases the sense of mastery. And this sense of mastery leads to even better performance. Management should therefore look to provide opportunities for early success in order to create the feeling of mastery necessary for ultimate achievement.

Some common sales motivation issues

Probably the best way to tackle this section is by answering some common questions about sales motivation.

How do we find out what motivates individuals?

This question was discussed above and various ways of eliciting this information through observation and discussion were mentioned. It should also be remembered that different things motivate different people at different stages in their lives, and that these things can change.

Is everyone motivated by incentives and targets?

People with high levels of achievement orientation are motivated by any kind of target. These people are simply motivated by meeting targets, irrespective of the type of incentive. In fact, just putting a target in front of such people is incentive enough.

Other people, however, do not respond to targets and incentives. To these people, such a motivational environment would be threatening and de-motivational. Although this is not common in sales, managers must be prepared to manage people who need to be motivated by different means.

Do financial incentives motivate?

There has been much debate over this, but it is probably true to say that money does motivate a large number of individuals in a commercial environment. Money can also be used as a measure of success, rather than merely as an incentive in itself.

However, not everyone will be motivated by money. In addition, managers should be aware that if sales activity is rewarded purely by financial incentives, such as commission only, then they should not be surprised if they attract and encourage people to pursue money single-mindedly, to the exclusion of anything else. This kind of financial incentive can thus encourage very aggressive and pushy sales behaviour, where the ends are seen to justify any means. This is the sales environment of the hit-and-run merchant, and management should question whether this behaviour, together with the customer reaction that follows, is what they want to promote?

If the aim is to promote high standards of behaviour, customer satisfaction and repeat business, then the organization should be looking to encourage activities that lead to these particular objectives, rather than out and out sales conquests. On the other hand, theory suggests that a straight salary does not motivate once it has become a regular and integral part of the overall compensation package. In such a case, a financial incentive or bonus would be necessary.

However, the theory also suggests that financial incentives eventually lose their appeal once people have sufficient money for their needs. How, for example, would you use money to motivate a footballer who earns £100,000 per week? The answer is that you probably couldn't. Such players are likely to be more motivated by being selected to play each week for a team containing world-class players that regularly competes for the highest honours in the game.

Are things like league tables, salesperson of the year and achievers' clubs a bit 'naff'?

They can be, but they are also an attempt to recognize, acknowledge and reward achievement, which is often highly motivational. Such things are also important in reinforcing the kind of behaviours considered important by the organization and in creating an overall culture of success.

How should sales targets work?

Sales targets should be seen to be achievable and ideally should have an input from the salesperson in their formulation. They should also be progressive and reward achievement at various intervals other than just at year end – perhaps monthly or quarterly. Any incentive should also be payable as close to the end of each period as possible in order to close the gap between effort and reward.

It is usual to pay incentives only at the 100 per cent achievement level, but in terms of motivation it is perhaps more effective to start paying incentives at around the 85 per cent level, to encourage a final push towards achievement. This is particularly relevant with stretch targets, where 100 per cent achievement represents a very challenging target. The stretch element of any target should reward exceptional performance and should be set on the basis of sales potential and not on historical performance. In addition to an individual component, targets should also have a group or team component to encourage team behaviour.

A word of warning: Targets that are considered unfair or that break the rules of equity outlined above can create more harm than good and be seriously demotivational.

Does motivation cost a lot of money?

This tour of motivational theory and the motivational framework developed above should illustrate the point that all kinds of things can motivate individuals. Giving people recognition and a sense of achievement can be the most powerful motivators, and may in fact cost the least amount of money!

Do motivators lose their power over time?

According to Maslow and his need hierarchy, once a lower-level need (food and shelter) is satisfied, people will strive to satisfy a higher-level need (status). If it is accepted that basic working conditions and a minimum salary allow employees to satisfy their lower-level needs, then the theory suggests that providing more of the same will not be motivational. However, going on to provide a sense of belonging and creating opportunities for self-fulfilment will become motivational.

It is probably also true that some tools of motivation, if over-used, lose their power. If, for example, the same competition is always used with the same prizes for the same level of achievement, then this is likely to lose people's interest over time and lessen the ability to motivate.

Can individual motivation get in the way of team or organizational objectives?

In the same way that purely financial incentives can promote aggressive sales behaviour, providing purely individual incentives can reward selfish behaviour at the expense of team or organizational goals. A group target and incentive, on the other hand, can promote team-working and the meaningful sharing of experiences, know-how and opportunities. All of this is very valuable to the organization and comes together to provide customers with a joined-up experience of dealing with the organization at various levels. Perhaps the aim should be a balance of motivational tools that reward appropriate behaviour and support the organization's way of doing business, while also supporting the objectives of its sales and customer strategy.

In this section the theories of motivation have been explored and related to the sales environment to create a *sales motivational framework*. In the final analysis, the factors that motivate individuals and groups are very specific to the individuals and groups in question. There is thus no substitute for getting to know a team and what makes them tick. Hopefully, the necessary tools and techniques have now been developed to do just that.

Workshops and case studies

A number of workshops and case studies can be found below. These are designed to help the reader apply some of the techniques discussed in this chapter and to illustrate how organizations have coped with some of the issues involved.

WORKSHOP   Development and Motivation Workshop 1:
Team development lifecycle

Objective

This workshop is designed to identify where the team is in its development life cycle, specifically to see which of the classic behaviours associated with *forming, storming, norming, performing* and *decaying* are being displayed. Management can then take the appropriate actions to help the team increase its effectiveness and thereby increase its performance.

Process

1   Reacquaint yourself with the theory of team development in the section on development earlier in this chapter, and particularly with Figure 8.4 showing the stages in team development.

2   Draw this diagram on a sheet of flip-chart paper and mark the stages from *forming* through to *decaying* on the curve.

3   Review the lists below that illustrate the typical behaviour of teams in the various stages of their development. This should help you to identify where your team is in its lifecycle.

4   Go back to the section on development again and consider the options available for management action to improve team performance.

Key behaviours

Typical behaviours in the forming stage:

- Nobody seems to listen to anyone else and people often talk at the same time.

- Individuals do not say anything if it might upset anyone else.

- Team members do not risk personal embarrassment and always play safe.

- Some individuals are clearly angling for control.

Typical behaviours in the storming stage:

- Team roles are not developed and individuals do not know where they stand.

- Individuals take sides to attack those with different views and ideas.

- Ideas are often attacked and rejected before they are properly considered.

- Individuals do not really listen to each other and misunderstandings easily arise.

Typical behaviours in the norming stage:

- A good leader of the team has emerged.

- The team realize the need for structure and formal processes such as agendas, objectives, individual contributions and timekeeping.

- There is less negative behaviour and more mutual trust.

- Individuals feel confident enough to make positive contributions to the team.

Typical behaviours in the performing stage:

- There is some flexibility around procedures and rules.

- Supportive behaviour rather than competitive behaviour is now the norm.

- Roles are well established and allow each team member to fully contribute.

- Team members are confident enough to participate and contribute in their most effective way.

Typical behaviours in the decaying stage:

- Outside influences are strongly resisted, especially those involving any changes to the group or its role.

- Rules and procedures are overly strict and constrain team flexibility.

- New ideas, concepts and different ways of working are discouraged.

- The team often looks backwards rather than forwards.

CASE STUDY Development and Motivation Case Study 1: Operator of telephone network – Conducting a training needs analysis (TNA)

Background

The company is a provider of voice and data services for the corporate and consumer markets in the Middle East and Africa. The expected entry of a strong global competitor into the organization's home market was causing the organization to review its strategies and objectives. The company wanted to establish a marketing academy to develop the essential marketing knowledge and insights across its marketing department. As part of this process, the company decided to undertake a training needs analysis to establish the current levels of marketing knowledge and skills across the department.

Activity

Meetings were undertaken with senior management in marketing in order to understand the strategic direction of the business and its vision, goals, market definition, distinctive competencies and competitive positioning. Meetings were also undertaken with senior management in HR in order to understand the organization's business purpose and in particular its culture, beliefs and values. Additionally, all members of the marketing department were interviewed to establish their level of marketing knowledge and experience, and to identify what additional marketing training they required to make them more effective in their specific marketing roles.

As a result of this TNA, a marketing academy was created to offer a range of marketing training modules, including strategic marketing, new product development, CRM and advertising/digital marketing. Individuals were then invited to the relevant module based on the assessment of their current marketing knowledge and their future requirements.

Key learning points

- Involving all marketing team members in the TNA created great interest in the establishment of the marketing academy and effectively pre-sold the involvement of individuals in particular marketing modules.

- A common vocabulary and understanding of marketing was created across the entire department, which greatly contributed towards effective communication and teamwork across the department.

- All managers within the department attended the modules, and then insisted on the marketing principles that were developed being used in all aspects of departmental work.

- As a result of the higher level of marketing knowledge and insight created across the team, many of the existing marketing objectives and strategies were reviewed and improved.

CASE STUDY   Development and Motivation Case Study 2:
Manufacturer of building materials – Developing field appraisal
and skills coaching

Background

The company had previously developed a competency profile of its salespeople that brought together the key competencies, and their constituent elements of knowledge, skills and behaviour. Additionally, a field appraisal process was developed to assess the effectiveness of salespeople against the standards of performance required for them to be effective in their role. The company wished to use this appraisal process to assess the performance of the sales team, but more importantly to raise the sales performance of the entire team, particularly lifting the average performers to the level of top performers.

Activity

All regional sales managers were trained in how to use the field appraisal process to assess and appraise salespeople, and in how to provide constructive performance feedback and skills coaching. A series of role plays were undertaken to allow the managers to practise giving and taking performance feedback from each other.

Thereafter, each salesperson was accompanied by a manager for field appraisal every 6 weeks in order to observe and review their performance in line with the competency profile that had been agreed by all parties. During the appraisal discussion, the salesperson was first asked to rate their own performance on each of the factors in the schedule and to identify their own particular strengths and weaknesses. The sales manager then either supported this self-assessment or made an alternative suggestion as to performance. A final rating was then agreed between the salesperson and the sales manager.

A plan of action was then agreed with the salesperson to exploit their specific strengths and/or to address their most significant weaknesses, either by asking them to mentor other salespeople or to receive mentoring or training themselves. This discussion and agreement was recorded for each salesperson in a personal development plan. During subsequent appraisal sessions, progress was reviewed against the previous personal development plan and any new elements requiring attention were discussed.

Key learning points

- The whole appraisal and development process was seen to be highly motivational by the whole sales team.

- Training the managers to appraise their staff in a positive and constructive manner was seen to be essential to preserve the developmental nature of the process, so that it was not perceived by the salespeople as merely a stick to beat them with.

- The creation of a positive climate of performance improvement was seen to be instrumental in the organization's growth and success.

CASE STUDY Development and Motivation Case Study 3:
Tyre manufacturer – Development of strategy coaching

Background

This company conducted a customer profiling exercise using the Customer Relationship Matrix to identify its most important customers and prospects (see Chapter 3 on customer strategy). Those customers identified as key accounts or development accounts were then account-managed using an account planning process that was common across the business. The company wanted to develop strategy coaching to ensure that these accounts received the focus and resources they were felt to deserve.

Activity

On the first Monday of every month, which became known as *Strategy Monday*, the sales director invited all account managers to a meeting, at which they were asked to present their key account plans and to discuss progress. All account managers were encouraged to make suggestions to each other as to how further progress could be made against account objectives. The sessions were skilfully facilitated by the sales director to ensure that discussions remained positive and focused on moving forward rather than looking back.

Key learning points

- The strategy sessions were seen as very useful by the account managers in sharing ideas and strategies about how to manage customers.

- The strategy sessions allowed managers to stay informed on the status of the relationship with their most important customers and best prospects.

- These strategy coaching sessions were seen as very constructive and very important in winning and securing business with the company's most important prospects and customers.

PART FOUR
Implementing Strategy

Implementing strategy

09

Priorities for action

In Part One of the book, the Business Performance Value Chain was introduced, which identified all the elements of sales and customer strategy necessary to win and keep customers in the B2B marketplace. Hopefully we have now established that all these elements are necessary for success and form part of an integrated performance framework. Any element that is missing will therefore have significant consequences for business performance.

FIGURE 9.1   The Business Performance Value Chain

Creating Strategy			
Strategic Direction	Customer Strategy	Value Proposition	Sales Process
Vision & Goals	*Customer Understanding*	*Total Proposition*	*Activity Management*
Core Competencies	*Relationships*	*Differentiation*	*Account Planning*
Market Definition	*Importance & Targeting*	*Customer Value*	*Structure*

Business Purpose
Culture / Beliefs / Values / Leadership

People & Performance
Roles / Structure / Skills / Objectives

Development & Motivation
Coaching / Rewards / Performance Feedback

Managing Strategy

BUSINESS PERFORMANCE

The Business Performance Value Chain emphasizes the primary status of those elements at the forefront of both creating and managing the strategy by emphasizing the creation of strategic direction and the development of business purpose. The role of management is therefore crucial in providing the organization with a vision of the future and the means to achieve this vision.

The self-assessment exercise was provided in Part One to enable readers to assess the effectiveness of their own sales and customer strategy in each of the areas outlined in the Business Performance Value Chain. In this section, we are going to pick up on this analysis in order to identify priorities for management action. It might therefore be a good idea to review the assessment you completed at the start of the process, or alternatively to complete it now.

The scoring system should enable you to identify your key areas of focus:

Creating Strategy

- strategic direction;
- customer strategy;
- value proposition;
- sales process;

Managing Strategy

- business purpose;
- people and performance;
- development and motivation.

The first issue that must be addressed is the scope of those actions needed to improve business performance, in particular whether these changes are *strategic* or *operational* in nature.

Strategic v operational change

A *strategic change* is one that implies a transformational change in any vital aspect of organizational strategy, whereas an *operational change* is more of a refinement of existing strategy. A strategic change requires detailed planning and communication and has wider implications for the organization as a whole, whereas an operational change can be confined to a much smaller area of organizational activity.

Those issues implying a strategic perspective are:

- a new strategic direction (vision, overall goals, market definition, competitive positioning);
- major changes to business purpose, culture or values;
- implementation of the notion of the customer experience driving all organizational activities;

- a range of new products or services being required;
- a major review of all customers to produce new customer targeting and customer profiling;
- a new sales process and sales structure, implying major changes to recruitment and development.

Those issues implying an operational perspective are:

- some clarification and better communication of strategic direction and business purpose;
- a greater emphasis on how the value of the product and service is communicated to customers;
- refinements to the customer strategy, particularly revised customer targeting;
- some minor changes to organizational structure;
- some minor changes to the reward system;
- some minor changes to the training and development plans.

In the final analysis, whether a change is strategic or operational is a matter of circumstances and management judgement. The self-assessment exercise from Part One should help to identify whether strategic or operational change is required and the specific areas of focus where these changes should be made.

Leading change

Whether managers are involved in leading operational or strategic change, a number of assumptions are offered to guide the change:

- Change is more effective if those who have to alter their behaviour or activities are involved in the change.
- Some of the best ideas about what to change or how to change come from those involved in existing activities.
- A facilitative approach, where leadership is provided to guide and support change, is ultimately more effective than an authoritarian decree.

These assumptions are incorporated into the two change frameworks outlined below for operational and strategic change.

Leading operational change

Operational change is more a case of refining what you already have than making wholesale changes to specific aspects of strategy or operations. The relevant parts of Part Two of this book (*creating strategy*) and

Part Three (*managing strategy*) should provide most of the necessary background and strategy frameworks to enable you to make the required changes to any aspect of sales and customer strategy. The following examples give brief outlines for how such operational changes can be made.

Refining customer strategy

If, for example, you want to refine your customer strategy, involve your sales team as follows:

1 Ask the team to use the Customer Relationship Matrix to position their customers in the appropriate boxes.

2 Ask them to use Customer Importance Mapping to identify their key accounts and development accounts.

3 Ask them to use the Customer Journey Framework to identify how their customers make buying decisions and who is typically involved at each stage of this buying process.

4 Ask them to create Customer Profiles for each category of customer.

Refining value propositions

If, for example, you want to refine your value proposition, involve the sales team in a workshop session as follows:

1 Ask the team to list all aspects of the total proposition using the framework outlined in Chapter 4 on the value proposition.

2 Ask them to use the Differentiator Matrix to identify the most important elements of the total proposition, which are likely to produce competitive differentiation.

3 Ask them to develop value propositions for each category of customer using the Value Proposition Creator.

Refining the sales process

If you want to refine an existing sales process or to introduce a new one, ask the sales team to consider the following:

1 Ask them to use the sales process part of the Customer Journey framework to define how each category of customer should be engaged.

2 Ask them to develop a sales funnel or sales pipeline for activity planning and to estimate the success ratios from one stage in the funnel to the next.

3 Ask them how they would use their sales funnel to create more accurate sales forecasts.

4   Ask them which of their customer relationships would benefit from account planning.

Developing competency frameworks/development planning

If, for example, you want to begin a process for developing competency frameworks and development planning:

1   Ask the team to list those competencies that they regard as important in successful salespeople.

2   Ask them to define the elements of knowledge, skills and behaviour upon which these competencies are based.

Further work will then be required to assess the importance of the competency elements identified in the workshop and to develop standards of performance, which should then be presented back to the sales team for approval.

The examples outlined above fulfil the assumptions made concerning effective change, in that they involve those who will ultimately have to implement the changes.

Leading strategic change: Lessons from consultancy

The following section is concerned with leading strategic change and draws on the author's consultancy experience in facilitating strategic change. This section will therefore be of keen interest to senior managers requiring strategic change in their organizations. It will also be of value to internal change agents or external consultants who wish to influence strategic change in commercial organizations.

A framework for strategic change

The following framework (see Figure 9.2) has been successfully used by the author to help organizations implement strategic-level change. Although practically based, it does reflect the key aspects of change management found in most books on this subject.

Building momentum and quick-wins

The key to strategic change within organizations is to create early success and quick-wins in order to generate a momentum of success. The analogy of a snowball gathering size and momentum as it rolls down a hill is a good

FIGURE 9.2   Leading strategic change: Lessons from consultancy

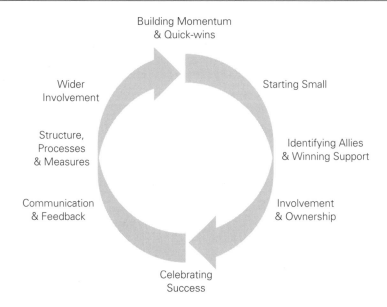

Building Momentum
& Quick-wins

Wider
Involvement

Starting Small

Structure,
Processes
& Measures

Identifying Allies
& Winning Support

Communication
& Feedback

Involvement
& Ownership

Celebrating
Success

one to keep in mind – getting the snowball to a critical mass and then getting it moving down the hill are the hardest parts of the process.

The best way to start is therefore to identify those early objectives that can be achieved relatively easily and quickly to help build this momentum of successful change. There are also significant advantages of starting in the right place at the right time. This means identifying an area of change that is most likely to result in success, rather than an area that presents significant difficulties.

Starting small

The saying 'Don't try to boil the ocean' could have been specifically written for those trying to effect strategic change within commercial organizations. Although it may be tempting to try and change everything at once, the sheer scale of the task, together with the inevitable complexity and complications, is likely to derail such grand plans.

It is probably better to start small with a specific group of people or within a specific area of the organization. This will enable efforts to be more concentrated and targeted on the key levers of change required to move this part of the organization forward.

Identifying allies and winning support

A change process cannot be undertaken by one person. It has to be embraced by a number of people who together make the change happen.

A key element in building the momentum of successful change is therefore to recruit allies and supporters to the change process, and for them to help move the process forward.

Figure 9.3 identifies the different categories of individual and their attitudes to change by comparing their *intellectual buy-in* versus their *emotional buy-in*. Intellectual buy-in exists where individuals accept the business logic of any change, whereas emotional buy-in exists where individuals have bought into any change and are actively involved in it. Successful change needs enough individuals that satisfy both of these conditions.

FIGURE 9.3   The Buy-in Matrix

Champions are the main allies and supporters of any change, as they are high in both intellectual buy-in and emotional buy-in. They accept the rational argument for change and are committed to being part of it.

Champions are important players in any change process because their actions and influence will be necessary to create the momentum of success referred to earlier. These important supporters are likely to be found amongst those with a personal interest in any new order or amongst those who are likely to gain the most from any change.

Bystanders have also bought into the rational argument for change but are not yet committed to making it happen. As such, they are not likely to help in building the momentum for change unless they can somehow be recruited to the cause. This might be by helping them to identify what they might gain from the process or end result.

Bystanders are perhaps the most problematic group to deal with, as they can sometimes claim to support the change without really meaning it. They are therefore difficult to identify until quite late in the change process, by which time their true colours are finally revealed.

Loose cannons have bought into being part of the change, but do not yet understand the rationale for change or its direction. These individuals can be useful in the change process provided they are given clear direction about what they can do to help the process. Loose cannons are therefore potential champions if handled properly.

Weak links have no intellectual or emotional commitment to any change and can therefore become serious blockers of any change process. They should be identified as early as possible in the process and prevented from getting in the way.

Involvement and ownership

This element is closely related to the overall change philosophy outlined above, which requires the involvement of all the key players in the change in order to create ownership of the eventual change measures. The best way of ensuring buy-in to these measures is to involve the key players right from the start and to use them to create the momentum of change.

Celebrating success

Building a momentum of successful change requires that any early success or early wins are recognized and celebrated. These celebrations will not go unnoticed by the rest of the organization, which will begin to feel excluded from all the fun and excitement. This is a very positive state of affairs as it will lead to those other areas of the business wanting to become involved in the change process in some way.

Communication and feedback

Change can create anxiety around the organization and a lack of information and feedback about what is going on can make this anxiety even worse. An important aspect of any change process is therefore early and regular communication on what is happening and its implications for the organization. This is particularly important if there is good news or a quick-win to communicate.

Structure, processes and measures

This element has been relegated to late in the process for good reason. In many change initiatives, organizations want to rush into making formal arrangements before the new behaviours and activities have been fully accepted.

A premature move to formalize new structures and processes will stifle creativity and bring the change process to a grinding halt. The momentum of successful change must therefore be well and truly underway before any attempt is made to impose formal processes or procedures.

Eventually, however, new activities and behaviours will need to be formalized in order to support any change and integrate these new ways of working into normal activity. Of particular importance are reward systems, which should support the change rather than working against it. Many a change process has come to grief by failing to recognize new behaviours and activities with new performance measures. A classic mistake is trying to encourage team-working within an organization, without developing some kind of team recognition or reward mechanism.

Wider involvement

Having built the momentum of successful change, there is probably a need to widen the area of involvement with the change by taking it into other areas of the organization. The overall process of change developed through this section will make such an extension of change activity much easier to achieve. The rest of the organization should now be ready to join what is perceived to be a very positive and exciting process.

10

The Art of War: A translation into sales and customer strategy
Sun Tzu

The famous Chinese General Sun Tzu wrote one of the world's oldest and most successful books about warfare. It might be interesting to see if someone who lived over 2,000 years ago can throw any further light on competitive strategy.

> **Important quotes from**
> ***The Art of War* by Sun Tzu (1)**
>
> *If you know yourself and your enemy and the terrain, you will win*
>
> *Be always ready to modify plans*
>
> *There is no instance of a country having benefited from prolonged warfare*
>
> *First put yourself beyond defeat, then think of defeating the enemy*
>
> *Rapidity is the essence of war*

We will look at each of the major quotes from the book in turn and interpret them in the context of sales and customer strategy.

If you know yourself and your enemy and the terrain, you will win

This point seems to suggest that insight into your own organization, coupled with an understanding of competitors in the context of the external environment are essential elements of success. This point allows us to revisit the most important aspects of the sales and customer strategy.

In *strategic direction*:

- Having a sense of *vision* – knowing where you want to go as an organization.
- Translating this vision into some concrete *overall goals* that confirm the organization is on the right path towards this vision.
- Knowing the *distinctive competencies* of the organization – what it is particularly good at.
- Defining that place in the market where the organization is going to compete.
- Having a clear sense of how to the organization should be perceived in the minds of its customers.

In *customer strategy*:

- Knowing who the most important customers are and identifying the nature of the relationship that the organization should have with them.
- Identifying the key accounts and development accounts.
- Knowing how customers make buying decisions.
- Creating *customer profiles* that detail all that is known about the most important categories of customer.

With the *value proposition*:

- Knowing all the elements of the total proposition and which of these elements provides the opportunity for competitive differentiation.
- Knowing how each element of the proposition can create value for the customer.
- Having a number of ready-made *customer value propositions*.

In *sales strategy*:

- Having a specific sales process for different categories of customer in response to how they buy.
- Understanding the key differences between *activity management* and *account planning*.
- Understanding business buyer behaviour and the various roles that individuals can take in the DMU.

- Understanding that some customers are likely to be more responsive to the organization and its proposition than others.
- Knowing the objectives, tradable elements and limits in any negotiation.

In *business purpose*:

- Knowing what the organization stands for and what it considers important.
- Knowing the difference between leadership and management.
- Knowing how leaders use culture to instil the necessary values and beliefs into the organization.

In *people and performance*:

- Understanding the constituent elements of performance.
- Knowing what kind of people will be needed and what they will need to be good at to implement the strategy.

In *development and motivation*:

- Understanding how a developmental philosophy can transform performance.
- Understanding the theories of motivation and how to apply them to different individuals.
- Understanding how to use strategy and skills coaching to improve sales competencies.
- Understanding the stages that occur in the development of teams and the management actions that are appropriate at each stage.

Be always ready to modify plans

This suggests that an organization's strategy should be flexible enough to respond to changes in customer requirements, to new competitive actions, or to changes in the external environment. When looking at strategic direction, the point was made that organizational flexibility and rapid response were perhaps even more important than an ability to predict an uncertain future. It would appear that Sun Tzu might agree. This of course assumes that the organization has a process capable of scanning the external environment for opportunities and threats.

There is no instance of a country having benefited from prolonged warfare

This might suggest that all-out war with a competitor should be avoided, as it would result in lower returns for both sides. This is not an argument for collusion, but it suggests that a more effective strategy might be to find a place in the market that can be defended and then developed. This would be a market niche that provides an opportunity to make the most of the organization's particular *strengths* and *distinctive competencies*, and allows it to win a specific place in the minds of its chosen customers.

First put yourself beyond defeat, then think of defeating the enemy

This point might support what Peter Drucker (a famous business writer) said about business: 'The main business of any business is to stay in business'. This rather suggests that the future survival of the organization is its most important objective. Given that survival can only be guaranteed by the ongoing support of customers, this would seem to imply that sales and customer strategy should be at the forefront of all management decision making and that any strategy that strengthens the competitive position should be implemented.

Rapidity is the essence of war

This point indicates that strategy and planning may well be important, but if these plans are not quickly put into action, any strategic advantage can soon be lost. This is a further argument for organizations to develop their flexibility of response in order to enable them to respond quickly to competitive moves or to changes in the external environment.

Important quotes from
The Art of War by Sun Tzu (2)

Supreme excellence consists in breaking the enemy's resistance without fighting

Concentrate your forces

If the enemy is superior, evade him

In order to defeat the enemy, our men must be roused to anger and have their rewards

Spies are essential to know your enemy's strength, disposition and plans

---

Supreme excellence consists in breaking the enemy's resistance without fighting

This point suggests that by demonstrating specific strength in a particular market or product area, or by signalling future intent, an organization might be able to deter competitors from launching initiatives in its chosen market space.

Concentrate your forces

This would imply that to try and be 'all things to all men' – that is, to try and cover all areas of the market with a wide range of products – could be a risky strategy, as it spreads organizational resources too thinly. Perhaps, therefore, an organization should concentrate on what it does best, by focusing on those aspects of its proposition that differentiate it from competition and by targeting customers that are more likely to respond to its product and service offering.

If the enemy is superior, evade him

This implies that an organization would do better to find a position in the marketplace that provides some freedom from competitive threat, rather than competing head-on with a stronger competitor or market leader. There is probably room for manoeuvre in most markets for smaller competitors to find their own niche away from the attentions of more powerful competitors.

In order to defeat the enemy, our men must be roused to anger and have their rewards

This would suggest that a major role for leaders is to instil a sense of passion and belief within the organization in its efforts to reach its vision and to achieve its overall goals. Additionally, managers should remember the principles of motivation and try to ensure that individual and organizational goals can coincide to produce maximum performance.

Spies are essential to know your enemy's strength, disposition and plans

Given that commercial espionage is not yet legal, this might suggest that organizations should at the very least look to understand their competitors, particularly their strengths, weaknesses and favoured competitive strategies. It would also indicate that organizations should seek to anticipate the likely competitive response to any aspect of their sales and customer strategy and not assume that their market activities will remain unnoticed.

Perhaps if Sun Tzu were alive today, he might have a new career as a business strategy consultant.

GLOSSARY

The terms below are found in this book and are defined as follows:

account management   Account management is a technique of managing customer relationships where there are a relatively small number of larger customers who are all important.

account planning   Account planning is a technique used to manage key accounts or development accounts by facilitating the development of strategy and monitoring the results.

account team   Account teams are groups of salespeople or other individuals working together on the same customer.

achievement orientation   Achievement orientation is a theory of motivation that relates to how much individuals feel compelled to achieve things.

activity management   Activity management is a technique of managing customers and customer opportunities where there are a large number of relatively small customers and all of these customers are of approximately equal importance.

advocate   An advocate is a level of customer relationship where an enthusiastic customer is willing to communicate their positive experience to other potential customers.

appraisal   Appraisal is the means by which managers assess the performance of salespeople, such as field appraisal.

approver   An approver or evaluator is part of the customer's decision-making unit. They test the product or service to ensure it meets requirements.

attitude   Attitudes are personal attributes such as diligence and professionalism, but the term behaviour is preferred in this book.

attribute   Sales attributes are knowledge, skills and behaviours and they are the building blocks of the sales competencies that lead to sales performance and sales success.

B2B   B2B refers to the business-to-business environment, where one business or organization sells to another business.

B2C   B2C refers to the business-to-consumer environment, where businesses or organizations sell to individual consumers.

behaviour   A behaviour is a personal attribute of a salesperson, such as diligence or professionalism. Behaviour can be learned and changed.

beliefs   Beliefs are a part of business purpose and relate to what the organization collectively perceives to be true.

benefit   A benefit is some advantage that the proposition or some feature of it can produce for a customer.

brand   A brand represents the entirety of what a business organization represents in the mind of customers and in the market generally.

business performance   Business performance is defined (in this book) as the ability to win and keep customers.

Business Performance Value Chain   The Business Performance Value Chain is a framework that identifies all the elements important in creating and managing sales and customer strategy – all of which are key drivers of business performance.

business purpose   An organization's business purpose defines the organization and everything it believes in. As such it can be defined as the essential reason why the organization exists.

business strategy   Business strategy includes a number of elements that come together in support of the sales and customer strategy, including manufacturing, operations, logistics, finance and HR.

buyer   A buyer or purchaser is a member of the customer's decision-making unit who has the final say in any purchase decision.

buying process   The buying process represents the various stages in a typical customer buying decision. It consists of need, search, evaluation, decision and review.

bystander   In organizational change, bystanders have bought into the rational argument for change but are not yet committed to making it happen.

call rate   Call rate is the number of sales calls made in a period, such as daily or weekly.

champion   In organizational change, champions are the main allies and supporters of any change as they accept the rational argument for the change and are also committed to being part of it.

change   Change happens when an organization needs to respond to the impact of the external environment, or when it is making any adjustments to its internal organization implied by its competitive strategy. A strategic change is one that involves a fundamental change in any vital aspect of organizational strategy, whereas an operational change is more of a refinement of existing strategy.

chunked-down goal   Chunked-down goals are when some overall objective is broken down into bite-sized chunks, such as by dividing annual objectives into 12 monthly targets.

client   A client is a customer who has developed from their initial position of new customer to a situation where they are now making further purchases or have started to buy additional products and services. In effect, the customer has moved to the level of repeat customer.

coach   In account strategy, a coach is a positive influence within the buying organization and supports the selling organization in the purchase decision by acting as initiator, sponsor, recommender, champion, friend, introducer, informant or winner. A coach is also an individual who helps others to improve their performance.

coaching   Coaching is where the competencies that are fundamental to sales success are developed. Skills coaching is where managers look to develop the necessary sales competencies, whereas strategy coaching is where managers help to develop account strategy.

collaborative relationship   A collaborative relationship with a customer is when the product or service has a high degree of complexity or uniqueness and where the strategic or cost impact of this product or service on the buyer is high.

competency/competence   Competencies are things that people can do. They are broadly based descriptions of overall capabilities and are made up from a combination of the different attributes of knowledge, skill and behaviour.

competency profile   A competency profile specifies what a salesperson must be able to do in order to be successful. It details the standards of performance for all competencies, knowledge, skills and behaviours and outlines how they are measured.

competitive positioning   The competitive positioning of an organization is how it wants to be perceived in the minds of its customers within its chosen marketplace.

consultative relationship A consultative relationship with a customer exists when the product or service is relatively complex or unique and therefore needs a significant amount of tailoring to meet specific customer requirements. However, the product itself only has a relatively minor strategic or cost impact on the buyer.

core competencies/distinctive competencies The core competencies of an organization are what it does best and they therefore define the uniqueness or special attributes of the organization relative to competition.

critical incident A critical incident relates to any situation where a customer has a specific issue with an organization during any touch-point with the organization.

culture An organization's culture is a collective term that describes what the organization believes in and what it values. It can also be defined as 'how we do things around here'.

customer experience The customer experience is what the organization wants the customer to experience whenever they come into contact with the organization.

customer importance mapping Customer importance mapping is used to evaluate different categories of customer to decide which customers are the most important.

customer interaction A customer interaction is any situation when a customer comes into contact with an organization for any reason.

customer intimacy Organizations focusing on customer intimacy will put a strong emphasis on providing customers with what they want and will seem to go out of their way to meet any reasonable customer requirement or expectation.

customer journey The customer journey is a framework that represents the various stages in a typical customer buying process. It consists of need, search, evaluation, decision and review.

customer lead A customer lead is a potential customer that must first be qualified before continuing along the sales process.

customer perception Customer perceptions are what customers believe to be true about organizations or their products and services. In marketing, it is said that perception is reality, which means that what customers believe is true for them.

customer portfolio Customer portfolios are created by allocating specified numbers of customers to the appropriate level of account manager or account executive.

customer profile A customer profile is a description of a specific category of customer and includes the customer's key requirements, buying process and the relationship required.

customer relationship management Customer relationship management (CRM) is a process for managing customer information and making it available to any individual in the organization to assist them in making an appropriate response to any customer issue.

Customer Relationship Matrix The Customer Relationship Matrix is a framework that looks to identify the different types of customer and the relationship they require. This is done by evaluating them on the strategic or cost impact of the purchase decision from the customer's point of view and the complexity or uniqueness of the proposition from the seller's point of view.

customer share Customer share is the share an organization has of a specific customer's business.

customer strategy The organization's customer strategy refers to the selection of those customers that have been identified as providing the best opportunities for the kind of business the organization wants to win and retain.

customer value proposition   A customer value proposition is the offer made to the customer, which consists of some combination of the product and service that creates value.

decaying   Decaying is a stage in a team's lifecycle where effectiveness is lost over time.

decision-making process   A decision-making process represents the stages a customer passes through during the course of their purchase decision and is the same as the buying process.

decision-making unit   The customer decision-making unit consists of all those individuals involved in the customer buying process and their relative positions and roles.

development   Development is about helping people give of their best and relates to such things as appraisal, coaching and training.

development account   Development accounts are potentially attractive customers that currently only provide the organization with a relatively small share of this attractive business. They are therefore key targets for additional business.

development philosophy   A development philosophy believes that anyone can develop higher levels of performance given the right encouragement and support, particularly through coaching and training.

differentiating competencies   Differentiating competencies are those capabilities that particularly separate the good performers from the less good.

differentiation   Differentiation refers to the way an organization's proposition is different in some positive way from competitive offerings to form the basis of its competitive positioning.

Differentiator Matrix   The Differentiator Matrix is a framework that allows an organization to evaluate all aspects of the total proposition to identify those that can provide it with competitive advantage.

early adopter   Early adopters are very similar to innovators and will be among the first individuals or organizations to respond positively to new product ideas and new ways of doing business.

early majority   The early majority are individuals or organizations with a conservative nature; they are less likely to try new products or new ideas.

elevator pitch   An elevator pitch is a short and punchy summary of the value proposition that could be given in a few seconds to someone in an elevator – hence the name.

ends   The ends relate to what the organization is looking to achieve in terms of performance.

engaging   Engaging is the second stage in the sales process that consists of opening, analysis/fact-find and summary/vision.

equity theory   Equity theory is a theory of motivation that suggests that people have a strong sense of what is fair and what is not, and that this perception will have a strong influence on how they perceive certain situations and how they respond to them.

expectancy theory   Expectancy theory is a theory of motivation that suggests that people are motivated when they can see a clear link between what they put in to something and what they get out.

external environment   The external environment consists of those factors impacting upon an organization that it cannot usually control: economic, political, social/

cultural, technological and competitive. These factors give rise to opportunities and threats in a SWOT analysis.

fact-find The fact-find is part of the *engaging* stage in the sales process, where the organization finds out as much as it can about the customer, particularly their business situation and their requirements and expectations.

feature A feature is purely a description of some aspect of the product or service.

field appraisal Field appraisal is the means by which managers assess the performance of salespeople when they are carrying out their role in the field.

field appraisal document The field appraisal document brings together all of the competencies and key sales attributes, with their definitions and their associated standards of performance, into one document. It is designed to be used by management to observe and assess sales performance.

finding The first stage in the sales process; it consists of searching, prospecting and qualifying.

forming Forming is the first stage of the team life cycle, when individuals find themselves members of a new team and expectations, objectives, roles and responsibilities are unclear.

gatekeeper A gatekeeper is an individual who is part of the customer's decision-making unit. They stand guard over the purchase process, either allowing or denying access to any aspect of the decision process.

goal Goals are the end results of strategy or vision.

goal-setting theory Goal-setting theory is a theory of motivation that says that individuals are motivated when they can work towards goals.

Herzberg's motivation–hygiene theory Herzberg's motivation–hygiene theory is a theory of motivation that seeks to identify what people like about their jobs (motivators) compared to what they dislike (hygiene factors).

incentive An incentive is an inducement to perform, such as a sales incentive to encourage a salesperson to achieve targets.

influencer An influencer is an individual or group of individuals who are part of the customer decision-making unit. They create the criteria by which any purchase will be evaluated, or otherwise influence any aspect of the purchase decision.

innovator Innovators are types of individuals or organizations that are the most eager to try anything new. They will be the first to respond positively to new products and services and to innovative ways of doing business.

input Inputs are the means necessary to create a specific output in performance.

intermediate performance measure An intermediate performance measure is a measure of progress that provides assurance that progress towards an objective is being made.

job description A job description lists the essential elements of a specific job role, its principal deliverables, how performance is assessed, and other aspects such as rewards and reporting relationships.

keeping Keeping is the final part of the sales process, where the organization is trying to keep the business during any customer review. This stage includes customer satisfaction, relationship development and added value.

key account   Key accounts are those customers that generate high levels of business and where the organization has a high share of this business.

key purchase criteria   Key purchase criteria are those factors that customers perceive to be important when making a purchase decision.

knowledge   Knowledge is a personal attribute and relates to what a salesperson knows about the market, their customers, their products and services, and about their own organization. Knowledge is acquired.

laggard   Laggards are individuals or organizations who are the sceptics of the marketplace. They are very unlikely ever to accept new ideas or new ways of doing business.

late majority   The late majority are individuals or organizations who are very conservative, and who will wait until others have tried new products or ideas before they try them themselves.

leadership   Leadership takes a strategic perspective of an organization's activities and is crucial in both creating and managing strategy. Leadership is normally delivered through motivation, coaching, development and the support of an organization's culture.

lifetime value   The theory of lifetime value states that the longer a customer remains a customer, the better for the organization, because the more business they will put its way, the more revenue it will receive and, hopefully, the more profit it will make.

loose cannon   In organizational change, loose cannons have bought into being part of any change but do not yet understand the rationale for change or its direction.

maintenance accounts   Maintenance accounts are customers that do not generate much attractive business, although the organization does pick up most of what business does exist, which it should try to maintain.

management   Management takes an operational perspective of an organization's activities and is primarily involved in ensuring that an organization's sales and customer strategy is delivered.

market definition   An organization's market definition refers to the particular markets within which it wishes to compete, or defines specific market areas or niches it wishes to target.

market share   Market share is a measure of how much of the available business is held by a particular organization in a given marketplace.

Maslow's need hierarchy   Maslow's need hierarchy suggests that people have a hierarchy of five needs that they seek to satisfy in a specific order of priority.

means   The means relate to how an organization proposes to achieve its performance objectives.

measures of success   Measures of success relate to the ultimate achievement of sales objectives and targets – how sales performance will be measured and how sales success will be defined.

mission   The term mission is synonymous with business purpose, but due to the confusion between vision and mission, the term business purpose is preferred in this book.

motivation   Motivation is a process that explains how people can be encouraged to adopt specific behaviours in pursuit of specific objectives.

negotiated relationship   A negotiated relationship exists with a customer when the product or service purchased is very important or fundamental to the buyer's business in terms of its strategic importance or its cost impact, although the product itself has low complexity or uniqueness.

negotiation A negotiation exists where two parties vary elements of their commercial position to secure an agreement.

norming Norming is the third stage in the team life cycle where roles and responsibilities become clear and the real work of the team begins.

objection An objection is where a customer raises a query or resists the closing stages of the sales process when the salesperson is trying to win the business.

objection handling Objection handling is where a salesperson deals with a customer objection in a satisfactory way as far as the customer is concerned.

objective An objective is a target for achievement.

opening The opening is a part of the engaging stage in the sales process, where a salesperson may meet the buyer for the first time.

operational excellence This is a value delivery strategy, where the organization has strong central authority and standard operating procedures. Such organizations are effectively process driven and allow very limited flexibility in any aspect of organizational activity or behaviour.

opportunistic account Opportunistic accounts are customers that generate little in the way of attractive business and what business they do create tends to go elsewhere.

order size Order size relates to the total size of the order placed or the range of different products sold per customer order.

Organizational Blueprint An Organizational Blueprint is created by identifying what the sales and customer strategy implies for the rest of the organization in order to deliver the required customer experience in terms of people, process and technology.

output Outputs are a measure of performance and relate to the end result from any given input.

overall goal The organization's overall goals relate to specific measures that indicate whether the vision is being achieved. Goals are therefore clearly defined and concrete end points of the vision.

ownership Ownership refers to when individuals adopt a strategy or action as their own, which makes that strategy or action more powerful and more likely to be implemented.

performance feedback Performance feedback is where results of performance are fed back to the performer to allow for improvement or to provide motivation for further action, such as in field appraisal.

performing Performing is the fourth stage of the team life cycle and is the ultimate goal of team development. It is where the team's output and performance reaches its peak.

personal development plan A personal development plan records the agreement between the salesperson and management as to how certain levels of performance are to be developed through coaching and training.

Position A An organization is in Position A if it is better placed than any competitor to win the business.

process A process is a prescribed way of carrying out a task or an activity. It is similar to a procedure.

product A product is the physical aspect of the customer proposition that creates value for the customer.

product leadership Organizations focusing on product leadership place high value on new ideas and original thinking in order to encourage the development of those new product ideas that are vital for their success.

proposition The proposition is the offer made to the customer, which consists of some combination of the product and service that creates value for the customer.

prospect A prospect is a qualified lead and therefore a potential customer.

prospecting This is an early part of the sales process that scans the marketplace for potential customers in the early stages of their buying process.

proving Proving is the third stage of the sales process where the salesperson provides evidence for how their proposition will create value for the customer.

psychological contract A psychological contract is a theory of motivation. It is an understanding that exists between an organization and an individual, where both parties receive something they value.

qualification A formula applied to all customer opportunities in order to evaluate their value and importance and to rate their overall attractiveness in order to decide if they are worth pursuing.

qualitative research In marketing research, a qualitative research study, such as a focus group, is a small-scale study where perceptions and ideas are explored.

quantitative research In marketing research, a quantitative study involves a large sample of respondents to enable any analysis to be statistically significant.

quick-win A quick-win occurs when a relatively easy gain has been made from any aspect of strategy or business activity.

recruitment Recruitment is where new people are brought into an organization.

reinforcement theory Reinforcement theory is a theory of motivation that suggests that rewards will encourage positive behaviours, whilst punishments will discourage negative behaviours.

relationship ladder The relationship ladder is a theory that suggests organizations should increase the level of relationship they have with customers in order to achieve business benefits.

relationship marketing Relationship marketing suggests that whereas the emphasis used to be on finding and winning new customers (customer catching), it should now shift towards developing customer relationships (customer keeping) in order to grow business.

sales force automation Sales force automation is similar to CRM as it provides the means to record all relevant customer information and customer transaction data in order to provide salespeople with accurate and up-to-date information.

sales funnel/sales pipeline The sales funnel or sales pipeline is a technique in activity management for identifying the progress of customers through each stage in the sales process, quantifying the success rate from one stage to the next.

sales organization The sales organization consists of the management and salespeople (the whole sales structure) responsible for sales performance.

sales performance framework The sales performance framework identifies all the elements that constitute performance from the means, through progress, to the ends. The framework therefore helps to identify what performance is and how it comes about.

sales process The sales process defines how the organization will engage with its target customers to reflect the buying process of these target customers. This process consists of finding, engaging, proving, winning and keeping.

searching This is the start of the sales process, where the marketplace is scanned for potential customers in the early stages of their buying process.

service A service is an element of the customer proposition that creates value for the customer. It sometimes supports a physical product but in other cases the proposition consists entirely of a service with no physical product at all.

situational leadership Situational leadership suggests that management action should be appropriate and proportionate to the situation faced.

skill A skill is a personal attribute. It relates to a specific ability of a salesperson, such as the skill of questioning to identify customer requirements. Skills are developed through practice.

spidergram A spidergram illustrates how the organization is currently positioned against customers' key purchase criteria. It also illustrates how the organization is positioned against competitors on the same dimensions.

standards of performance Standards of performance are what the organization expects in terms of the various competencies and knowledge/skills/behaviours important in determining sales success. They are therefore benchmarks by which performance is judged.

storming Storming is the second stage of the team life cycle, where team members better understand the nature of the overall team tasks, objectives and expectations. They also begin to clarify roles and responsibilities within the team.

strategic direction The organization's strategic direction refers to the overall vision and goals that pull the organization forward, together with the organization's distinctive competencies, market definition and competitive positioning.

strategy Strategy is the means to achieve a goal or objective.

strength Strengths relate to what an organization is particularly good at relative to the competition. They are the same as distinctive competencies.

stretch objective A stretch objective is a higher target for achievement, which hopefully motivates an individual to achieve more.

strike rate Strike rate is the ratio of calls where an order is taken to total sales calls.

structure An organization's structure is a combination of the different types of people necessary to implement strategy and how they work together.

summary The summary is part of the engaging stage in the sales process, where the salesperson summarizes what they have learned of the customer's situation.

supporter A supporter is a customer who is enthusiastic about everything the selling organization does.

SWOT analysis A SWOT analysis brings together the threats and opportunities that exist in the external environment, together with the specific strengths and weaknesses of the organization.

target A target is a sales objective given to a salesperson.

team life cycle A team life cycle relates to the stages that a team goes through following its initial formation, which include forming, storming, norming, performing and decaying.

terms of engagement Terms of engagement relate to what management expect from salespeople and what salespeople expect from management.

territory A territory is a geographical area containing a specified number of customers, where a salesperson is expected to achieve a sales target or other objective.

The Art of War The Art of War was written about military strategy by the Chinese General Sun Tzu over 2,000 years ago.

Theory X/Theory Y Theory X and Theory Y are theories of motivation that suggest that there are two basic but contrasting assumptions about human behaviour.

Theory X is largely negative in how it views human behaviour and Theory Y is largely positive.

total proposition   The total proposition is the entirety of the organization's product and service offering. It represents the whole package of everything made available for customers, out of which customer value is created.

touch-point   A touch-point relates to any situation where a customer comes into contact with an organization.

trading value   Trading value is where a salesperson adds or subtracts elements of their customer proposition as part of a commercial negotiation.

training   Training is a formalized process of developing any aspect of competence or any element of knowledge, skill or behaviour.

training needs analysis   A training needs analysis (TNA) is an assessment of performance against specified performance criteria in order to create a development and training plan.

transactional relationship   A transactional relationship exists when the customer only needs to acquire a product or service in a simple way at a low transaction cost.

user   A user is an individual or group of individuals in a decision-making unit who will use the product or service in question.

value   Value is the measurable advantage that a specific benefit can bring to a specific customer. Values are also elements of the organization's business purpose and can be defined as what the organization collectively perceives to be important.

value balance sheet   The value balance sheet is a technique used to represent the situation in the customer's mind where they consider both sides of the purchase equation; its costs and potential gains.

value delivery strategy   A value delivery strategy is a particular way that organizations compete in their marketplace. They include operational excellence, product leadership and customer intimacy. An organization's value delivery strategy and the organization's culture should be in alignment.

value mapping   Value mapping lists all elements of the total proposition (which are in fact features of the proposition) and looks to identify as many ways as possible that they can each create benefits and customer value.

value proposition   A value proposition is the offer made to the customer that consists of some combination of the product and service that creates value for the customer.

value proposition creator   The value proposition creator is a tool used to develop any number of different value propositions for different customers.

vision   The vision represents the overall aiming point of the organization – a star on the horizon that pulls the organization forward.

vision of the future   Providing the customer with a vision of the future is the final element of the engaging stage of the sales process, where the salesperson paints the idealized solution to the customer's issues.

weak link   In organizational change, weak links have no intellectual or emotional commitment to a change and can therefore represent serious blockers to any change process.

weakness   An organization's weaknesses are what it is not particularly good at, relative to the competition.

winning   Winning is the fourth stage in the sales process and consists of objection handling, trading value and negotiation.

INDEX